PARIS

R. Seine

R. Marne

Fontainebleau

St Mammès

Canal du Loing

Montargis

Canal de Briare

R. Yonne

R. Seine

Joigny

Canal de Bourgogne

Auxerre

Briare

Canal du Nivernais

Dijon

R. Saône

Marseilles les Aubigny

Nevers

Canal Lateral à la Loire

Canal du Centre

Chalon-s-Saône

Digoin

Tournus

R. Seille

R. Saône

R. Rhône

Lac Léman

R. Loire

Lyon

R. Rhône

Orange

Avignon

Nîmes

Beaucaire

Tarascon

Étang de Thau

Canal du Rhône à Sète

Arles

Agde

Sète

Aigues Mortes

Petit Rhône

Camargue

Marseille

MEDITERRANEAN SEA

Amsterdam

Lee

Sne

Zn

Arnhem

Deventer

Zutphen

R. Rhine

Dusseldorf

Köln

Approx: Scale
80 miles

R. Moselle

Metz

Toul

Nancy

Canal de L'Est
(South Branch)

Épinal

R. Rhein

Canal du Rhône au Rhin

Basel

3

TRAVELS WITH 'LIONEL'

TRAVELS WITH 'LIONEL':
a small barge in France

HART MASSEY

with illustrations by John Verney

LONDON
VICTOR GOLLANCZ LTD
1988

FOR MELODIE

First published in Great Britain 1988
by Victor Gollancz Ltd
14 Henrietta Street, London WC2E 8QJ

Text © Hart Massey 1988
Illustrations © John Verney 1988

British Library Cataloguing in Publication Data
Massey, Hart
  Travels with 'Lionel': a small barge in France.
  1.Inland navigation—France   2. France
  —Description and travel—1975–
  I. Title
  914.4′04838   DC′29.3

  ISBN 0–575–04175–7

Photoset, printed and bound in Great Britain by
WBC Bristol and Maesteg

Contents

Why don't we buy a barge?

It was very dark along the river and raining hard as our taxi pulled up at a wall above the quay at the end of Place de la Concorde decanting us on to the wet sidewalk in a kind of Parisian no-man's-land. A mist curled over the river, then in full flood, its turbulent waters covering the quays and making access to the moored boats hazardous. The owner of the barge we were to see had given us careful directions about how to reach his boat and, in the pelting rain, we set about following them as best we could like blind people groping in a strange place. By feeling along the wall with our hands Melodie and I at last found the ladder he had mentioned poking up from God knew what below. It disappeared quickly out of sight into the gurgling water but this was the described route and over the wall we went.

Nervously descending the shaky ladder we arrived moments later at what the owner had called a bridge, a grandiose word for what was nothing more than a springy, unstable and very narrow plank spanning between the ladder and the deck of some large, indeterminate craft. France is known for many things but safety awareness is hardly one of them. In spite of such insouciance, however, the little 'bridge' was fitted with token 'railings' of knotted string, perhaps intended more to bring home the hazards of the crossing than prevent the unwary pitching down to an uncertain fate below. As we crossed the plank, the precarious relationship between our feet and the flimsy construction required so much of our attention, it was only at the last moment that we saw a dark figure looming ahead of us. It was the owner of the barge.

We were about to take our first steps in an entirely new kind of boating game. For the previous six years my wife Melodie and I had rented small boats for relatively short holidays on the waterways of Europe. These boats gave us much pleasure and experience but are small and expensive to rent. We were both ready for a fresh challenge and came to a quick decision when, one day, Melodie said: 'Why don't we buy a barge?' The barge we were about to board on the Seine was one of the first candidates in what we then felt might be a long search for 'our boat'. The choice of a barge, rather than some other kind of boat was made for a number of reasons. We wanted a boat that would be suitable for the inland waterways of Europe; a boat that would conform to their limitations and stand up to their occasional hard knocks, a boat roomy enough for the two of us and our Dalmatian, Joss, to live on comfortably for several months at a time, a boat of moderate cost. These conditions pointed to a barge because barges are certainly designed for the medium in which they spend their working lives and are just as certainly roomy by nature. The idea of a barge also meshed with our own preference for the rough and ready working vessels of the continental waterways over their pleasure-loving distant cousins in the fancy world of yachts.

Barges, being load-carrying craft, tend to be big, heavy, cumbersome and slow. The problem of speed didn't matter much as long as our barge, like most of its kind, had enough power to breast the swirling currents of big European rivers even in times of flood. But weight, size, sheer awkwardness and whether we could handle a boat with these characteristics gave us some concern. Admittedly, running a barge has less to do with the age and brute strength of its crew than it does with skill and knowing what to do in any given situation, but both Melodie and I were now in our sixties and felt a little apprehensive. Our concern about this, however, had been greatly eased after a chat on the quay at Sens with two Americans then living on and running their own eighty-foot barge. Neither gave the impression of being in exceptional physical shape and both, we guessed, were in the further reaches of late middle age. If those two were able to deal with the demands and whims of such an ungainly iron beast, so, it seemed, might we. From that moment on we discounted age and flabby muscles as limiting factors in the coming adventure.

The first step before starting the search for our boat was to prepare a skeleton specification covering its desirable qualities. It was very short and to the point: length, beam, type of hull, location and height of wheelhouse (important for bridges), accommodation needed, maximum speed, engine type, hydraulic controls, plumbing, central heating, water and fuel storage tanks, electrical system and so on. There wasn't much detail, due in part to my ignorance of the subject but also because I thought it a mistake. Perhaps no boat could ever meet all the requirements of a detailed specification so it seemed important to keep it simple and retain some flexibility.

What we were looking for was a relatively rare commodity, a small barge fifty to seventy feet in length. Barges of this size were usually Dutch-built and used in the early part of this century for small commercial jobs on the canals and rivers of Holland. When road and rail transport took over that function the smaller barges were converted for other uses, many of them falling into private hands. Hardly any are now being made and they have become scarce, particularly in France where very few come on the market. Their rarity has also made them expensive, sometimes even more so than their larger commercial brothers. But, at first, we thought, if any were to be found, Holland would be the place to look.

Although Holland is certainly bursting with boats of every imaginable kind and barges may be cheaper there, something else must be borne in mind if the boat is finally to be based and used in France. A foreign registered boat may enter France and be used there for a maximum of six months, at the end of which it must either leave the country or its papers be surrendered to the *douanes* and the boat laid up for the next six months. The other option is to import the boat into France, paying the value added tax of 18.6 per cent on the value of the boat as established by the *douanes*. Naturally all this can be avoided if the boat is already registered in France. But in spite of the French import tax, a Dutch boat may still be less expensive than one bought in France and, in Holland, the choice is vastly greater. Much depends, however, on the state of the boat when it is imported into France. A barge in its original, bare-bones working condition may only demand a relatively small payment of tax whereas that on a luxuriously converted one can be exorbitant.

More by chance than anything else the first rather cursory search for a barge began in France. Recalling a few likely spots there from our hire-boat days, we stopped to look in the commercial barge town, St Jean de Losne, then in Dijon and Auxerre. Only in the last did we find a barge for sale, a large, expensive craft, which we did not find tempting. So on to Paris we went.

Paris seemed to hold out more hope. Surely here with all the barges lining the quays of the Seine there must be at least one right for us. In those days the Touring Club of France was still in existence, with mooring facilities and a small office on the Seine at Place de la Concorde. A notice-board in the office was covered with advertisements announcing boats for sale and the name of a Paris boat-broker who several weeks later was to play a key role in bringing our search to an end. Although I made a note of his name at the time we were then more interested in looking at boats. Disappointingly, there was only one, not very promising, possibility. It was this boat, a barge called *Bruno*, that we were now about to board on the darkest and wettest of Paris nights.

Bruno was moored on the outside of another barge which we now had to cross. This meant walking twenty-five yards or so along its narrow deck to the bow and back down the other side. In retrospect this sounds simple and I suppose it would have been in daylight, on a dry day with some foreknowledge of the boat's topography. None of these conditions prevailed at the time. The deck was narrow, slippery, booby-trapped with odd projections, ropes and hoses, and unguarded by railings. Later we became used to this kind of thing but there on that rainy night it racked the nerves. After gaining *Bruno*'s wheelhouse we were all at last able to see each other and the young owner immediately took us below.

I don't really know what we expected to find at the bottom of the stairs but it was certainly a great surprise to me. After the tricky passage through the dripping gloom, the arrival in the *salon* of the barge was a dramatic event. There opened out in front of us an enormous and sophisticated living-room that looked as if it had no business being on a barge at all. It was an amazingly generous space with a high ceiling and walls covered in eighteenth-century wood panelling removed, we were told, from an old Dutch church. There was a large wood-burning fireplace at one end of the room and a painting hanging above it, probably nineteenth century, but for all the attention I was paying to such details, could well have been a Rembrandt. My first reaction to all this was wonder that so much space existed inside a barge and that the room could have been lifted bodily from some old Parisian house. The young couple who lived in the barge were bright, well-educated, attractive, possibly high-born, fluently bi-lingual and quite clearly not impoverished. They entertained us simply and, in the French way, formally. They showed us over the boat which, after the *salon*, could not but be anticlimactic with major planning flaws apparent as we went from room to room. The only bathroom in this otherwise luxurious boat was at the stern, a good eighty feet from the master bedroom in the bow, an arrangement the inconvenience of which was dismissed by our elegant hostess who remarked: 'You get used to it.' And perhaps, if you're French, you can rise above such things. But this barge, with all its elegance, was not for us, being far too big and way beyond the upper limit of our price range.

Finding no more barges to look at in Paris we left for Amsterdam. There I obtained the names of several boat-brokers and studied as best I could the advertisements for boats in the Dutch papers. One of these, *Schuttewaer*, devoted entirely to boat matters, looked particularly useful, but not unnaturally required some knowledge of Dutch. I also went in search of a broker specialising in barges, wandering up and down Damrak in the rain without finding the office and finally sprawling painfully across tram-tracks in the middle of the busy street. I returned tired, wet and bruised to the hotel to continue my search later under the shelter of Melodie's umbrella, walking past the cheap hotels, fast-food joints and sex shops of Damrak until I finally found the broker's office and handed over my skeleton specification. Time, by then, was running out and we returned to Canada from where I began an active correspondence with all the boat-brokers and sat back to await developments, intending to return to Holland in the spring to start the search in earnest.

Information soon began to arrive from all my European contacts.

Most of the boats being offered departed too widely from our requirements or were too costly, but in February 1982 the Paris broker reported having a boat that might be right for us. In March we were again in Amsterdam. We had arrived early in the morning at our delightful little hotel on Herengracht to find our room not yet ready and were having coffee and biscuits in the living-room of the old house that now served as a kind of parlour for the hotel. Melodie sipped some coffee and then started rummaging noisily through her handbag. This seemed to go on for a long time. Then I heard, 'My God! I think I've left my teeth on the plane.' In the elegant atmosphere of that old Dutch room it was a startling announcement. But as so often happens, they weren't lost at all and, thankfully, Melodie was again able to face the world fully equipped.

A day or so later we got up at dawn to drive to Paris. Five hours after leaving Amsterdam we were driving along a road between the Seine and the Bois de Boulogne with the suburb of St Cloud climbing up the hill across the river. A boat, the spitting image of the one in the photograph we'd been sent, was moored in a marina on the far side. Melodie remarked on this: 'Oh, that must be the boat over there. Doesn't it look nice.' I had by then lived with this woman for thirty-four years and should have been warned. I suppose I have always been a little slow to read the signs and thought nothing of what she had said at the time. Later, I came to realise that I was the target of a carefully calculated 'soft-sell' campaign of which this remark may well have been the opening shot.

The boat, the law and *liquide*

Arriving at the marina, little more than a narrow strip of land separated from a busy road by chain-link fencing and locked gates, we plainly saw the boat moored below but could find no way of penetrating the barricade. Only by flailing our arms in their general direction were we able, at last, to catch the attention of the owners who let us in. Even after the long drive from Amsterdam, we had arrived on the dot for our rendezvous but there was no sign of the boat-broker, a key man in any subsequent negotiation. He finally wandered in forty-five minutes late after the relatively short trip from central Paris. The owners of the boat seemed greatly impressed by the discrepancies in arrival time compared to distance travelled, but I doubt if the credit we thus gained had much effect on our future discussions. Once assembled, we were all given lunch on board by Corinne and Jean-Luc Dandurand, a middle-aged, bourgeois couple who had used the boat more as a dwelling than a means of travel and were now anxious to unload the cramped quarters they had been enduring so they could live in a house again. Their dream, perhaps more hers than his, was to open a fish restaurant in the Auvergne and they hoped, I imagine, that we might be their means of realising it. They were an oddly matched pair; he, a lightly built, shortish, dapper man with a moustache, reserved in manner, perhaps a little wary, and his wife, plump, warm, talkative, an excellent cook and made up, as some middle-aged French women seem to be, with a thick beige foundation, heavy eye-shadow and shiny red lips that give them an incongruously sexy look.

At first glance the boat appeared to be, in very general terms, what we were looking for. It was Dutch-built in 1922, registered in France, had a steel hull sixty feet long by thirteen feet wide with enough space inside to provide the accommodation we wanted. The six-cylinder turbo-charged DAF diesel engine was certainly powerful enough and, if the owner was to be believed, gave the boat a sizzling speed of fifteen miles per hour. The interior was pure French, do-it-yourself kitsch, having been cheaply converted in bits and pieces by previous owners, its 'Mickey Mouse' appearance relieved here and there by feeble little efforts to recall something of a lost French *grandeur*. I found all this depressing, knowing only too well how much work would be needed to tear it all out and start again. But my limited knowledge and a cursory examination of the boat led me to think that the basics, at least, were satisfactory. I spent the next few days going over it in more detail, taking measurements and asking questions. My ignorance, however, made me terribly vulnerable and, although I didn't know it then, much of what I was told was either inaccurate or untrue. And my own unfamiliarity with barges led me to overlook problems that would later prove costly to correct. The lesson in this is obvious: if you don't know much about barges, get help from someone who does.

Melodie was blind to all the problems and wildly enthusiastic, captivated especially by the kitchen and the wheelhouse. The former seemed to me run of the mill but the wheelhouse was certainly a potent selling point, being large and full of light. Not many barges have wheelhouses like this, most being small business-like affairs. But this one was like an extra living-room, a marvellous place to sit and watch the changing scene outside.

Reaching the final decision was not easy. There were good arguments for and against buying the boat. It was almost the first one we had looked at, certainly the first of the right size and surely, I thought, there must be others even more suitable to be found in Holland. On the other hand, a search there might take months before the perfect boat was found, if such a thing existed at all. After all, the boat was fundamentally right in all important respects and French-registered to boot. Certainly a lot of work needed to be done but when it was finished the boat would be the way we wanted it. The pros and cons went back and forth for hours.

My reservations still persisted, however, for I knew that old hull contained hidden problems demanding money and months of work to put right. And most of that load would fall on my shoulders. Melodie lightly waved my worries aside and renewed with fresh vigour her sales campaign, now no longer 'soft' but hardening rapidly. She pointed out the undeniable truth that we were no longer young and could hardly afford to spend another year or more wandering about Europe looking for the ideal boat. 'Let's get on with it,' she said and I felt my resistance beginning to crumble. There was more than a whiff of commonsense in this view and, in retrospect, I know she was right. We could have wasted valuable time and perhaps never found a boat that so closely fitted our needs. But, alas, I was also right. It did take months of work and a seemingly endless flow of cash to bring our boat at last to a satisfactory state. Even about that, however, there should be no regrets for that is the price a boat-owner must gladly pay.

So, right or wrong, we decided to buy the boat. An offer was made, below, but probably not far enough below, the asking price. It was speedily accepted, probably confirming those fears. Although I would not wish to make it a dominating principle of my life, there are times, and this was one of them, when I would give anything to be the hard-nosed, calculating negotiator I am not. Business acumen has never been a strong quality in my make-up and, more often than not, in such dealings I feel like an innocent among thieves. The boat very probably could have been bought for far less, but my life has been spotted with incidents in which I have bought too high or sold too low. It is just the way things are with me and there seems no recourse but to resign myself to the unfairness of a fate that pre-determines I am, more often than not, on the losing side.

Before buying a boat it is prudent to examine the large area of hull that lies hidden beneath the water to ensure against leaks or other unpleasant surprises. This is a specialist's job that must be done with the boat out of the water. The purchase of the boat was, therefore, conditional on it being taken to a local boatyard for a thorough examination and arrangements duly made. That was simple enough but the legal, financial and even ethical matters that followed the offer to purchase were not. The first agreement of sale was drawn up by the laid-back young boat-broker, Alphonse Dufresne. A casual and likeable fellow in his thirties, Alphonse spent what must have been an entertaining, if insecure, life juggling the purchase and sale of an extraordinary range of boats all the way from little cabin-cruisers through a very mixed bag of yachts and barges to obsolete submarines. When not deeply enmeshed in complex boat deals he lived the carefree life of a slightly impoverished Parisian bachelor, roosting temporarily, when we knew him, with his ladder-climbing dog, in an ancient wooden barge tied up near Place de la Concorde. And it was there that we found him one afternoon typing with one finger the first agreement of sale.

For all his nonchalance I was inclined to trust Alphonse more than some of the players in the game but, even so, he was acting for and being paid by the other party to the deal. In the circumstances it seemed advisable to have someone involved who would look after my interests exclusively and, heaven knows, it was needed. In Canada I had obtained the name of a good Paris lawyer who, thankfully, turned out to speak some English. It was this man who steered the whole transaction along the right professional track, discarding with a laugh the agreement typed by Alphonse and preparing one of his own that was eventually signed by both parties.

The matter of payment proved to be more difficult and, to my mind, highly questionable. Because France taxes its citizens in motley irritating and exacting ways, the French have raised to a fine art the game of tax evasion. This shows itself in small ways and large. Many artisans and small businesses work in the black economy to avoid the cost and troublesome paperwork involved in the 18.6 per cent value added tax. In larger transactions, like buying a house or a boat, there is a commonly accepted, but illegal, practice of demanding part of the payment in cash or *'liquide'* to allow the seller to avoid, I suppose, a capital gains tax. Even one of the previous owners of the boat, a Commissioner of Police, had apparently insisted on this ruse.

But, early in the negotiation, I was still in ignorance of all this, although there had been much use of the words *liquide* and *confiance*. There was certainly a need for trust on both sides but the recurring mention of *liquide* was mystifying and it only dawned on me later that the current owner, Monsieur Dandurand, was insisting that a large chunk of the payment must be made in cold, hard cash – folding paper money. But even more than that, he wanted the sale price shown on the agreement to be only 60 per cent of the actual price. This struck me, an innocent Canadian lad, as highly unusual to say the least if not a good deal worse. I was greatly worried at being involved in this kind of thing and talked to my lawyer about it. He seemed to be only mildly amused at the proposed fiddle, accepting it, I suppose, as the way things are often done in his country and in reply to a query from me said: 'It's more illegal for him than for you. You are only a little guilty.' It was not exactly what I wanted to hear. I don't like being even a 'little guilty' and disliked intensely being trapped in a French boondoggle from which there seemed no way out.

This evasion of the law by the owner created legal problems as well as distress in the purchaser. Under any law, French included, the price shown on the agreement of sale is the only legal price. Consequently, once the document is signed, there is no obligation under law to pay more than this price, leaving the seller unprotected if that price is lower than the actual one. And there appeared no way that the cash part of the payment could be left in the hands of a third party to overcome the problem. If in the lawyer's hands he would be breaking the law and in anyone else's there was clearly no safeguard in the case of loss or theft. The best solution, the lawyer thought, was to wait until the boatyard inspection was carried out and, if all was well, make the entire payment then.

By this time, Melodie had gone back to Canada and I was not only disturbed by the murky manoeuvring but now found life in St Cloud becoming tiresome. My hotel had lost whatever appeal it once might have had. My room had become a bleak, uncomfortable cell, the dining-room held no further surprises for me other than the screw and washer it served up one evening in a chocolate mousse. I became fed up with the ants on the breakfast tray in the morning as well as the silver fish that crawled out of the bathroom walls each night. Even the occasional expeditions into Paris failed to stimulate as they once had. It was a good day, therefore, although dull and overcast with a cold wind blowing down the river, when we departed for the boatyard with both Dandurands, their son and daughter-in-law on board. Alphonse, the broker, would join us there later.

We set off downstream, coming soon to the only lock on the short trip. It was big, one of three side by side needed to cope with the heavy traffic on the Seine. There were a few ladders on the lock wall but Dandurand stopped the boat where there were none. I thought this a mistake but said nothing. I scrambled ashore to take the ropes with which there was a lot of ineffectual business. After several tangled bundles had been thrown vaguely in my direction I managed to grab one, sort the mess out and put the rope around a bollard. Having done that I was standing on the lockside admiring the lines of the boat as it lowered in the lock, delaying my return until it was almost too late. The only way to get back on the boat was a jump of seven feet, far more than I would wish. But I jumped to save the honour of Canada, hitting the deck hard, half-expecting to go through it and slapping my hands painfully on a skylight in an attempt to take up the shock. I hope that I concealed the pain and made the whole thing look as easy as pie.

After the lock I was allowed for the first time to take the wheel. It was a great tonic for me to be in control of a boat again: the boat itself had become a living thing at last, not the static steel artefact it had been in the marina. I stayed at the wheel until we reached the boatyard, where huge barges crowded the shore with more on land resembling beached

17

whales. It was not easy to see how we could even get close enough to be pulled out of the water but a slow shuffling of the barges allowed us to sidle in and position the boat over trolleys running on railway tracks into the water. Once high and dry we all examined the hull carefully. It appeared in reasonable shape but proper testing would tell the tale. The propeller, however, was badly damaged and the bottom pivot of the rudder needed repairs. It was Alphonse who brought this last defect to my attention with the quiet request that Dandurand not be told he had been my informant.

By the next day the hull had dried, been scraped down and, when I arrived, was already being tested by an inspector from the Port Autonome de Paris. Spots were selected all over the hull, ground down to bare steel, greased and the steel thickness measured with a sonic device. Apart from a little welding on the hull and repairs to the propeller and rudder the boat was declared in good shape. Then the hull was tarred and the job was done, the costs being split between the buyer and seller, the latter paying for the necessary repairs and the former footing the bill for pulling the boat from the water, scraping and tarring the hull. Perhaps not surprisingly, in view of what fate seems to reserve for me, the latter costs were by far the larger.

Leaving the boatyard that day I was nearly another kind of loser. I had already had one confrontation with the boatyard dog, a large, paranoid brute who eyed with dark suspicion all but the familiar figures of the workers. One day before on a visit to the boatyard office I was met at the top of the steps by this snarling giant. On the point of deciding that my business in the office could easily wait for another day I was saved from humiliating retreat by the timely arrival of a welder who calmed the dog. But the next time I had to run the gauntlet the workers had all gone home, the dog was running loose in the boatyard and I was entirely on my own. This dog had already savagely bitten Alphonse and I was far from keen to share his fate. Before making my dash for safety I waited until the dog was behind some machines deeply involved in marking the boundary of his territory. Then, at the crucial moment, I made for the gate, very quietly, with quickening pace and as much dignity as conditions allowed. But it wasn't much. To go from the boat near the shore to the exit at the road a hundred yards away demanded a kind of stooping walk-come-run under the great flat-bellied barges in various stages of repair and over a complex obstacle course made up of a random lacework of pipes, power cables, hoses, woven steel wire, railway tracks and miscellaneous bits of metal. To add to the hazards black tar was everywhere, underfoot and on the boats above. As I finally made my escape through this ferrous jungle I thought briefly of the Dandurands living in the boat perched high above the boatyard mess and deprived of all amenities, even that of plumbing. They could not be much enjoying their enforced confinement.

Now that the boat had passed its boatyard test, the agreement of sale could at last be signed. This was done and I gave Dandurand a cheque for the amount covered in the agreement. But in spite of all his talk of *confiance*, there was a certain lack of trust in the air. Still worried about his damned *liquide*, Dandurand explained that it was the normal custom in his country for the *liquide* to be handed over first. Since this had not been done he demanded an I.O.U. for the cash. I could see his point but I was, by now, getting fed up with the man and his illegal ways. I gave him what he wanted and set about finishing the matter by getting the *liquide* forthwith.

I consequently made arrangements with my bank in Paris to have this large sum available and made a special point of requesting them to be most discreet in the way the money was handed over to me since I had no wish to publicise my departure from the bank laden down with French banknotes. Arriving at the bank near the Opéra, I went to see my contact, the ice lady, businesslike Madame Morisette who worked at a desk in full view of anyone doing business at the tellers' counter. Before I could repeat my request for discretion, Madame Morisette began ostentatiously removing the banknotes from two large brown envelopes on her desk and started counting them. I was shocked and complained loudly but by then it was too late. Hurriedly making out the necessary cheque, I stuffed the bulging piles of notes inside my shirt where they nestled uncomfortably but I hoped securely and prepared to face a threatening world.

Outside, long familiar rue Scribe had suddenly become enemy territory. I left the bank feeling like a frightened deer marked for killing. Was that man casually reading a newspaper about to tail me? Why were those two across the road looking my way and muttering quietly? I hurried down the street, making for the Métro, hoping to be lost in its crowds. No one appeared to follow me and I began to relax. I had lunch somewhere but all I can remember about it was the *liquide* giving my bare stomach little pricks from time to time. Back at last in the boatyard I climbed the flimsy ladder up to the boat with a bottle of champagne and all the *liquide* stuffed into a little pot meant to be a

19

joking symbol of the Dandurands' new restaurant in the Auvergne. But the feeble gesture fell quite flat. I gave the pot to them with an explanation of what it was supposed to mean but there weren't even polite smiles as Dandurand snatched it out of my hand and rushed below to count the money. So much for *confiance*.

Moments later we tore up the I.O.U. and parted company to meet later at the marina aboard the boat. Here there was more champagne brought by Alphonse who arrived with an American friend sporting a red beard, plum-coloured fingernails and white-framed dark glasses attached to a white plastic chain around his neck. We all sat on the deck in the warm spring sun drinking the champagne and feeling good that the whole drawn-out, tricky business had finally come to a happy conclusion. Melodie and I had our boat almost before a serious search had even begun, Alphonse had his commission and Dandurand had his *liquide*. We were all happy in our separate ways. I then left them and drove to the airport.

Insurance

Even before consummating its purchase I had made the bus and Métro trip into Paris in search of a company to insure our new boat. I foresaw no great problem in this; insuring a boat would not be a very complicated matter and I felt sure there must be a number of companies dead keen to have the business. Certain in my own mind that it was only a matter of making a good deal, I advanced optimistically on the insurance industry of France, expecting to be welcomed with open arms. The reality couldn't have been more different. What had started out as an expedition to find which of several companies offered the best terms turned into a weary trudge from door to door in an attempt to find even one that showed the slightest interest. I visited five in all. The first refused to insure foreigners. The second, a famous British firm, claimed French regulations prevented them from insuring any French boats. The third only insured very small boats. The fourth rapidly lost interest when told the boat might be rented or lent to friends. But in this last office, at least, there was a kind and understanding man who was himself a boat enthusiast. This man telephoned five other insurance companies, finding one, at last, that would deign to consider our problem.

It was this last company, the ninth, which finally agreed to insure the boat . . . at a price. There were, in fact, two important catches, but by then in a weakened state, all fight had gone out of me. The premium was not only excessive but a clause inserted in the policy required me to pay a daily surcharge whenever the boat was moving. I accepted this reluctantly since the boat would be stationary for the next few months but later it was to become a curse. Whenever a departure was delayed or a voyage held up for any reason, I had to inform the Paris insurance company, often with some difficulty from remote rural telephone booths. After the first year I abandoned this French company and gratefully switched my custom to a small concern based in the west of

21

England. The premium dropped by about half and the new company had a pleasantly relaxed attitude to the whole business with not even a mention of surcharges or any such nonsense.

Initiation in St Cloud

Gilles Charrier was a taciturn fellow in his mid-thirties exuding an air of professional competence, reinforced no doubt by the pipe in his mouth and a reputation as a boat expert. Certainly his gentle manner and aura of quiet efficiency inspired a trust that would be needed in the coming weeks, especially so because of the inexperience of a new owner who had to take much on faith. Gilles had been recommended for the work by Alphonse, the boat-broker, but as is the case with so many men who earn their livelihood working on boats Gilles was not really a professional in the true sense at all. He proved to be only an amateur, most of whose work had to be redone later by others, also amateurs. But that is another story. For the moment I believed in Gilles, in his knowledge of boats and in his ability to perform.

The wheelhouse was the biggest and most complex of the jobs he had to do. The one already on the boat was a fixed steel affair, too high for many canal bridges. I wanted, instead, a wood demountable wheelhouse, a very common practice on commercial barges, though ours would be larger than normal, increasing the complications. In addition to this, Gilles had to install a new 5,000-watt generator, a battery-charger, battery-box and modify the antiquated engine controls.

Gilles and I had long stumbling talks about all this in French which, with me, is halting at best and then further restricted by a tiny technical vocabulary. In an effort to overcome the language hurdles Gilles and I spent many hours trying to synchronise our understandings of the problems and their various solutions. Sitting across the table in the wheelhouse, he would launch into an explanation of some technical matter and at the beginning, more often than not, this would be met by a look of blank incomprehension from my side. He would then start again using different expressions and slowly I would grasp, or think I grasped, what he was saying. The reverse process was somewhat similar. Using what I felt was quite lucid French I often saw an equally blank look on his intelligent face. But gradually my French and my technical vocabulary improved and we were soon able to tackle increasingly subtle matters. By the time I flew back to Canada in July I was certain that Gilles knew what he had to do. I gave him a small advance to buy materials expecting that work would soon get underway. How wrong I was.

Arriving in France again that autumn, I found the boat unchanged and no work started. This is, I suppose, the typical lot of the absentee owner but I lit a small fire under Gilles who soon got going. I also set to, with wild enjoyment, demolishing much of the awful interior, so cluttered with partitions and strange bits of do-it-yourself carpentry that there was very little free space left. In what would normally have been the *salon* there was even someone's idea of a Napoleonic four-poster canopy bed. It was one of the first things to go and it was followed to the scrap heap by a varied assortment of tacky shelves, tables and benches. Soon the *salon* started to look spacious with light pouring in from the windows. With the carpentry jungle partially cleared away, the hoped-for roomy and comfortable living space made its first promising appearance. It was a good moment.

The following day I was up before dawn and on the road to the Paris airport where Melodie and Joss, our Dalmatian bitch, were due to arrive at seven-thirty. There was fog along the way and after reaching the airport at six o'clock I found that all flights had been diverted to other cities: Melodie and Joss were to land at Frankfurt. The Arrivals level at Charles de Gaulle airport is always cramped and often in a shambles even at the best of times but, as the fog cleared and planes began arriving at about one p.m., it was soon plugged with mountains of baggage and shifting, shoving crowds of tired travellers. All pretence at customs control was abandoned and I wandered freely back and forth through the forbidden zone in my search for Melodie. In the crush I almost despaired of finding her but through the cacophony of noise I heard a faint but familiar voice calling my name and there she was, exhausted and on the point of tears. It was then a further hour before the bags and Joss, in her travelling cage, finally appeared. It must have been a dreadful trip for both of them but for Joss, especially unpleasant. Air travel is never nice for a dog but she had been cooped up in her cage for thirteen hours, mostly in dark, strange surroundings, spooked from time to time by scary noises and the last five hours on the ground in Frankfurt with little water in the intense heat.

Finding two luggage carts in a forgotten corner I assembled our lumbering caravan of carts, bags, cage, dog, tired wife and set out for the parking lot on an upper level where I'd left our rented car. Arriving where I was certain the car had been left, the little blue Samba was nowhere to be seen. Melodie and Joss stood limply looking at me, confidence in their leader draining rapidly away. It was not a good moment for any of us. But a rather panicky search brought the car to light and well down on its springs it carried us safely through the whirling Paris traffic to the sanctuary of our new home on the Seine.

For the first time we settled down to live on the boat which had been given a new name. We had considered the possibilities at great length, rejecting all the trickier ones, and finally settling on *Lionel*, the name of my brother who, we thought, would have liked the idea. It has the advantage of being the same in French and English and, although male, is quite at home on the European waterways where barges carry names that are sometimes male, sometimes female and often have nothing to do with either sex.

This was to be our first long experience of living in France. The boat was moored in the marina where we had first seen it, squeezed between the busy Seine and an equally busy road. The latter was not the finest feature of the place but the mooring had other things to commend it. Beyond the road climbing up a hill was the suburb of St Cloud, one of the more select residential enclaves on the outskirts of Paris, its houses increasing in size and opulence as they neared the summit. On the opposite bank of the river was the deep green mass of the vast Bois de Boulogne, the great forest park of Paris. Upstream a bridge carried traffic over the river to Porte de St Cloud and very close downstream, on a *passerelle* high overhead, pedestrians sauntered between the right and left banks of the river. Beyond this, in the far distance, the tall office towers of the development called La Défense poked into the sky like oversized *campanili*.

But the real delight of the place was the life on the river itself. The Seine carries a lot of traffic, boats of all kinds moving up and down throughout the day and the barges continuing after dark. There were tugs, work boats, yachts on their way to the south, huge tankers, motor-cruisers off for a week-end down·river, water-skiers, kayaks riding the bow waves of lumbering barges and on week-ends an additional flurry of sailors, windsurfers, rowers, speed-boaters and yet more water-skiers. And although St Cloud is outside their normal beat, the occasional *bateau mouche* or tour boat would drift by in the evening, brightly lit like a display case, its passengers eating dinner or dancing to a band . . . a gay, strange and unexpected sight on this businesslike river. But the river was really owned by the barges and it was they that held our interest as they passed in a constant stream: 350-tonners from most of the countries of western Europe, even Switzerland, 1,350 ton giants, immensely long pusher trains of four barges tied end to end and the leviathans of the river, the huge and powerful pushers churning up the water behind a floating cargo of 300 Renault cars on their way downstream from Billancourt to Flins. Sometimes a barge would pass bearing the name of a Canadian province and I discovered that these, like others we saw later on the Rhône, had been given by Canada to France to help her recovery after the Second World War. And also coming down the river was the inevitable floating detritus of a large city. It formed multi-coloured, undulating rafts in the quieter backwaters along the shore near our mooring . . . the unpleasant gift of this otherwise stirring river.

Because of the river activity we spent a lot of time in the wheelhouse. It was one of the best features of the boat and, at that time, about the only place one could sit, almost all else being in a state of partial demolition. We had a kitchen that barely functioned, a *salon* that was unusable and two beds, of a sort. It was, however, in the area of plumbing that the deficiencies were most irksome. It was an oddly balanced arrangement. We had two basins with cold, and occasionally hot, water. There was a bidet on a raised platform in a room with no door. The cantankerous WC worked sometimes but mostly didn't unless encouraged with a bucket of water. There was no shower or bath but this was a French boat and did after all have a bidet. The absence of shower or bath was a problem in the insufferably hot September of 1982 and there were times at night, lying in bed hot, sweaty and sleepless, one longed for some relief. Swimming in the Seine was unthinkable but we had a hose and, driven out by the heat we sometimes stood naked on the deck to hose ourselves down with delicious cool water from the St Cloud water system, putting out of our minds for the moment the people on the *passerelle* nearby. In their way these rough and ready ablutions were more enjoyable than any shower and we returned to our beds refreshed and perhaps a little cleaner. Later Melodie became over-conscious of the possible spectators on the *passerelle* and would appear on deck bottomless but wearing a long black T-shirt, 'Black Cat Café' writ large across its front.

Life aboard *Lionel* soon began to take on a pattern. Progress on the work remained abysmal. Although I wasted much effort to increase the pace Gilles had his own way of working and there was little I could do to change it. When not involved with Gilles I happily demolished more of the interior and spent time getting to know the boat. But I also came to know intimately the Paris suppliers and ship chandlers in numerous excursions to buy equipment of one kind or another. Ship chandlers are a vice with me. I can be triggered by the slightest pretext to embark on a long, involved journey just to visit one. I became familiar with many of these expensive places over the following weeks to order a new anchor, buy a dinghy, new ropes, boat-hooks, a refrigerator, two stainless steel singing kettles, bits of boat hardware, knives, forks, spoons and a myriad of other tempting things, some of which we really needed.

Relaxation took the form of walks with Joss in St Cloud or across the river in the Bois de Boulogne where we would sometimes sit under the trees watching the horses, with their colourful burden of jockeys, pound around a bend of Longchamp racetrack. Sunday was a special day and the three of us nearly always climbed up the hill in St Cloud to the little weekly market. There, we could buy couscous or paella, quail, a piece of fresh salmon or pigeon, which became a favourite with us. Joss found these market expeditions exciting, her senses almost

spinning out of control from all the sights, smells and snatched tidbits. My efforts to control her had little chance of total success and although she won a few rounds in this running game, she luckily always failed in the more daring form of it. Walking home behind women fresh from shopping with the inevitable stick of bread protruding from their baskets posed a temptation Joss could never resist. With my attention on other things she would manoeuvre within sniffing range but just short of the final nibbling phase. It was at that moment that the *baguette*'s owner and I were both alerted to the danger and took prompt action. Although we found much amusement in these sly stalks the homeward-bound shoppers strangely didn't seem to share it.

In the course of familiarising myself with every nook and cranny of our new craft I had come across a locker in the bow reached by steps from the deck above. It was filled with junk. Parking the discovery in the back of my mind, I put off dealing with it until, inevitably, the day finally arrived when I could no longer shirk the task. It was a dark, damp place that had become a home for an unbelievable mess of things. I steeled myself, opened the hatch, descended the shaky wooden steps and looked about me.

Apart from the anchor chain which nestled here in a flaccid heap, the bow locker must have been the place where all previous owners had found it expedient to stash everything that they didn't have an immediate use for but felt sure might come in handy some day and didn't have the guts to throw out. Piled in nasty scattered heaps were paint cans, some empty, some full but now quite useless, old deflated inner tubes with bits of stringy rope attached, plastic pails with mysterious, dried residues, old hoses, bits of wire, a bucket of rusty nuts and bolts, rubber-boots half full of water, an old fisherman's anchor, assorted bits of wood and metal, an incomplete stovepipe, a broken TV antenna, a dirty garden umbrella advertising Byrrh, plastic jerry-cans, wooden steps, a garden seat, odd lengths of shock cord, a steel towing cable, extra cordage of poor quality, countless containers minus labels with unknown liquids for unknown purposes, a case of empty beer bottles and at the bottom miscellaneous little heaps of just plain 'things'. As well, over in one corner, there was a bulging black object that looked like the dried skin of a small whale. On deck in broad

daylight it seemed more like a rubber sea-anchor, if such things exist. But the man I gave it to was sure it was meant to collect rainwater. He may have been right. In any event he was as glad to have it as I was to get rid of it. Perhaps he was in the early stages of stocking his own bow locker with useless things. It gave me pleasure to help him on his way.

Although the completion of Gilles' work never seemed to get closer than some hazy, indeterminate future time, a little progress was becoming evident. He must have sensed my growing exasperation with the slowness of it all but our relations were still good and we had drinks together in the wheelhouse at the end of most working days. He had now cut off the upper part of the old steel wheelhouse with an angle-grinder in a very messy, noisy and fiery operation but the old roof remained propped up to give a little, but not much, weather protection. When it rained water poured in on all sides but even when dry the wheelhouse was quite unusable. The only place now remaining where we could sit was a dark corner of what would someday be *Lionel*'s salon. We had reached a low point in our life aboard. There still lingered all the faults and deficiencies willed on the boat by others in the past and *Lionel* was now further disrupted, with no compensating reconstruction as yet in place. It was only barely possible to live on board at all, but we soldiered on knowing that matters would soon improve. It was at least comforting that much of the new equipment had finally arrived, including the new generator, a very heavy lump of Italian engineering.

Joss had adjusted well to the new life aboard *Lionel*, even managing the steep stairs without trouble although her descents always seemed a shade out of control, being a kind of galloping near-fall salvaged at the last moment by a face-saving leap. We took her for frequent walks but the marina itself offered no more than what amounted to a three-hundred-yard-long concrete walkway beside the water, interrupted in the middle by the office and repair sheds. The French are pretty understanding about the free-wheeling ways of dogs and will put up with far more than most in those places dogs share with people. But Monsieur Charpentier, the proprietor of the marina (dubbed by Melodie the Taipan of St Cloud) was not so tolerant and made it clear that the splendour of the place was not to be sullied by Joss even though his own two black poodles sullied away like anything. This meant that whoever took Joss for a walk had to cope with events as they unfolded. It was never easy and mishaps occurred. Melodie reported one morning that she had casually flipped the offending matter over the high chain-link fence enclosing the marina. But her aim was off and, as she watched helplessly, it landed on the windscreen of a parked car belonging to an employee of the Dassault Aerospace Company across the road. There was little she could do but hope that the owner of the car would have enough fortitude to face the ghastly mess confronting him at the end of a hard day's work.

The new windows for the wheelhouse started to arrive at last. They were also the walls as well, since the wheelhouse was largely glass. Every one had to be sanded, varnished, sanded again and varnished twice again. It was a big job and a long one, keeping us busy almost to the time we left St Cloud. Each window had to dry for twenty-four hours between coats, and they all had to be covered or brought inside at night or if rain threatened. It became a tedious business and, because there were a lot of windows, they were sometimes left lying all over the boat in various stages of completion. Joss, whose only really strong urges in life are eating and a yearning to be close to Melodie and/or me at all times, felt very deprived of that contact when we were both working on top of the roof over the salon where many of the windows were lying flat and freshly varnished. Wandering around unhappily on the deck below she came, at last, to a decision and in one great leap arrived in our midst, wagging her spotted tail as she padded slowly over glass and wet varnish to say hello to each of us. I let out a scream. Joss looked offended, and sensible Melodie calmly led her away from the danger zone. If you looked closely, her paw-marks could still be seen on the wheelhouse windows many months later.

During the days at St Cloud I tried as best I could to get at least on nodding terms with the various systems – plumbing, electrical and mechanical – that were *Lionel*'s vital functions. After a while it became clear that these systems would only bring their basic truths to my attention through little dramas of their own making and, sometimes, minor disasters of various and troubling kinds. These incidents seemed to occur most often in those early days when I tried to run something, fill something or pump something out. The first drama involved the bow water-tank which I was filling with a hose and not paying much attention, assuming there must be an overflow somewhere. A little later I was down below and noticed with alarm water bubbling up through the floor and running down the corridor. I did not, for the moment, connect this strange phenomenon with what I had been doing and summoned Gilles to the scene. He looked at the water, said: 'C'est bizarre!' and quickly withdrew to resume his work. This didn't strike me as helpful but I soon reached the unbelievable conclusion that the overflow of the water tank was INTO THE BOAT and immediately turned the water off. Since then I have found that this peculiar arrangement is not unique to *Lionel* but is found, oddly, on many barges.

The stern tank played a similar trick on me. Although I should have been more cautious, this tank had been dreadfully slow to fill and I felt safe leaving a hose running while I went to a local store. When I came back after a few minutes, the tank was still not full and I became suspicious. Of course it too had overflowed, this time flooding the engine-room. I then began to think that the filler pipe of this tank was at least part of the problem and decided to investigate, finally discovering a sixteen-inch-long, wooden-handled carpenter's rasp lodged in the neck, effectively reducing the passage to a fraction of its full size. It was anyone's guess how it had got there, and when I showed it to Dandurand he made no comment, nor, I think, saw the funny side of it. One problem thus solved, I installed a proper overflow and this tank now became our principal source of water, although it was still connected to the bow tank which we didn't use because of the rusty water in it. I had one day done a silly thing by opening a valve which allowed the rusty water to pollute our entire water system. This didn't please Melodie. The pots and pans were all rust-stained. Even the food started to look brown and, to drive the point home, Melodie showed me an egg that had cracked in boiling. The escaped 'white' had turned dark brown. The valve has remained closed ever since.

Our time at St Cloud was now running out. In November we were to meet a carpenter in Auxerre who would rebuild the interior of the boat, but Gilles was still far from finishing his work. I was anxious and started to apply pressure, in response to which Gilles acquired a young assistant. This only slowed matters still further, Gilles having to spend much of his time showing the boy what to do. Although the work was 90 per cent complete the final 10 per cent seemed unattainable. Our departure was delayed several times more by Gilles' inability to keep to deadlines and the previous owner's son, Claude, who had promised to join us for two days of the voyage south, had to rearrange his life each time the plans changed. It was embarrassing for us but he steadfastly stood by his commitment.

Now that we were on the point of sailing, my time was occupied in getting the boat ready for the voyage. In the engine-room there was much I had to take on faith, believing it would work but hardly understanding any of it. I had a manual for the DAF diesel, the main engine of the boat and had often crouched beside it with the manual in my hand comparing the photograph in the book with the actual thing. No matter how long I studied them, the two looked like quite different engines. I remained perplexed by this. The engine was a Chinese puzzle of pipes, valves, wires, pumps and odd appendages, the purposes of which were then unknown to me. I thought the only way I could deal with these mysteries was to treat the diesel like the motor of a car. I would feed it the right liquids in the right places at the right times, turn the key to start it, carefully monitor its vital signs, move the controls as required and hope for the best. It certainly looked sturdy enough to run the boat and, probably, withstand a little abuse from me. On the deck the huge and cumbersome fisherman's anchor was attached to the anchor chain and placed for rapid deployment in an emergency (a most unsatisfactory arrangement later changed.) Ropes were put in coils where they would be needed and rubber bumpers hung over the side to protect the hull in the coming locks. The larder was stocked, nine bottles of wine stowed away and, except for Gilles, we were ready to go.

Gilles was still plodding on, now working at night as well as during the day with his useless assistant. The final stage in building the wheelhouse roof was a fiddling, fussy business with much measuring, fitting, cutting and cursing. Gilles looked haggard from the long hours of work but the end seemed no nearer. We were all, I suppose, under a strain in those last days but the crew's morale was greatly improved by the arrival on board of Claude Dandurand who stayed to work on the boat and immediately injected into the atmosphere a notion of, and belief in, imminent departure. Even Gilles must have sensed that this was finally IT and speeded up as best he could. The next morning we would leave and there could be no further delay. Claude and I helped Gilles put his unfinished work in a state that would allow us to travel and, although no one in the marina expected us to go, we were now quite determined to leave St Cloud. In the late morning Claude and I moved to the quay all the tools and materials that had been littering the boat. When this was done, we said goodbye and Gilles disembarked. As we pulled out of the marina he was standing on the quay, looking a little surprised and waving sadly, beside a mountain of tools, bits of old wheelhouse, lumber, steel, wire, our old refrigerator (now his) and a bottle of wine. It was the last time we saw him.

Maiden voyage

It was a fine moment when we pulled out of the marina at St Cloud. After nearly two months tied to a dock and enduring disruptions of every kind, *Lionel* vibrated with life and eagerness to be on the move again. With the big diesel chuffing away beneath my feet we eased carefully into the Seine current and turned upstream towards Paris. This was my first time solely in charge of what was to me then an enormous craft. Over the previous six years I had driven many smaller boats starting with something that was nothing more than a tacky box on two thin pontoons and moving on from that waterborne joke to the normal plastic hire boats of Europe. But *Lionel* was quite different. In barge terms, of course, it was not a huge boat but the bow, some fifty feet from where I was standing, still seemed a long way off. I approached the new task with caution, some trepidation and not a great deal of confidence.

The afternoon was warm, sunny and fortunately windless. I was grateful for the last since as a virgin captain I had no wish for the added challenge wind was certain to throw my way. The river was a smooth, silky grey as we made our way slowly upstream through the heart of Paris. It was a gorgeous journey: past the newly refurbished Eiffel Tower, with the École Militaire at one end of the long formal axis and the Palais de Chaillot across the river at the other. Then through the centre of Paris, Place de la Concorde, the Louvre and, best of all, Île St Louis and Île de la Cité, those two precious islands in the Seine. One-way traffic around the islands brought us through the south channel past the Palais de Justice and almost under Notre-Dame which towered magnificently above us. The imperatives of the busy river, however, forced us on past the great cathedral, Île Saint Louis and into the main channel again. Then the centre of Paris slipped astern and I had to face my first moment of truth as captain of *Lionel* . . . a docking.

At this crucial moment, memories came back of the humiliating shambles we had made of our first-ever boat docking six years before in

Ontario. We had tried so hard to do it properly but a brisk off-shore breeze and rank inexperience conspired with the mad design of the boat to set the scene for a grade A marine fiasco. The sequence of events had gone something like this: *Captain* bumps *boat* clumsily alongside dock. *Crew* leaps eagerly ashore with rope no. 1. *Crew* ties rope no. 1 to bollard with *knot*. *Captain* throws rope no. 2. Rope no. 2 too short. *Crew* dashes to rope no. 2. Rope no. 2 slides off dock into water. Rope no. 1 unaccountably unties its *knot*. Rope no. 1 slithers across dock to join rope no. 2 in water. Wind blows *boat* away from dock and *crew*. *Boat* drifts out to sea, both ropes trailing in water, *captain* standing speechless at wheel.

Now, six years later, there was to be another first docking. We were low on fuel and, for the journey south to Auxerre, would need full tanks. The fuelling dock, when found, looked, and was minute, no more than four to six yards long, a flimsy wooden floating affair, more appropriate for rowing-boats than a sixty-foot barge. But this was the only place and it had to be faced. Natural caution, fears about the effects of river current and unfamiliarity with the habits of the new boat led me to approach the dock warily and dead slow, the latter always a golden rule. It certainly worked this time. Beginner's luck perhaps but even after several years' driving this boat I could have done no better, coming alongside without a jolt and the only sound a gentle kiss of rubber. It was then late afternoon so a little further on we moored for the night in an industrial suburb of Paris near the junction of the Seine and the Marne. It was not a nice place. The quay, a desolate, débris-strewn concrete shelf beside the intake of a municipal waterworks was, however, in spite of its shortcomings, a kind of paradise for Joss whose bladder, by this time, was close to bursting.

Next morning we awoke to a light grey world of near zero visibility, a dense fog hanging damply over the river. It would have been folly to continue that day and we reluctantly had to say goodbye to Claude Dandurand whose promised two days would expire that night. After spending a few minutes talking by radio to other barges about the extent of the fog he left with our grateful thanks to return to his work and family. As the day dragged on, three barges came to moor nearby: *Monza*, *L'Éspoir* and *Nelly*. Others, more daring or foolhardy, drifted slowly past, barely seen through the fog, radar antennae whirling or, more often, the shrouded figure of the captain's wife peering ahead through the murk from her outpost in the bow. On closer acquaintance our mooring turned out to be even nastier than when first seen. Rising up from the twelve-foot-wide concrete dock was a stone wall sloping up to a road far above where construction of some kind was in progress. Every so often cans, bits of paper and plastic would be thrown over the wall by persons unknown, to come bumping down to the quay where they joined us and the odd white-footed rats which shared our mooring.

It was not a place to stay so, in spite of some remaining fog, we were glad to get away the next morning, shortly to face our first Seine lock. These are large, electrified, efficient and, like all European locks, give priority to commercial traffic. This can often entail waiting while the working barges are passed through but, if lucky, one can sometimes shadow a barge and go into the lock with it, greatly accelerating progress. Loaded barges are normally too slow to make following one worth while but that day we got behind an unloaded barge moving at close to our maximum cruising speed. Only just able to keep up with our trail-breaker we went through lock after lock with this barge, albeit at some expenditure in fuel because of the speed we had to go.

I suppose, not surprisingly, since *Lionel* had been stationary for several months, the stress of travel soon found weak points in some of its systems. On that second day of cruising, as the boat slowly approached the entrance to a lock, an alarm buzzer on the instrument panel suddenly burst into vigorous life. All sorts of wild and panicky thoughts swept through my head for I knew that the buzzer was an alarm for low oil-pressure, a serious business in any internal combustion engine. What had gone wrong? Oddly enough the buzzer had never worked after it was installed at St Cloud, so the fact that it was now buzzing must mean something, and probably something serious. I looked at the oil-pressure gauge. It appeared normal. The buzzer continued to shout its warning. I touched it. It stopped. Why? Could it be playing weird little games with the new captain? I took the engine out of gear and pushed the throttle forward. The oil-pressure increased as it should and I knew that all was well. A little later I removed the playful little buzzer, never again wanting to be scared out of my wits in this way.

That day was marked by two further crises of a lesser kind. Purely from whim I decided to visit the engine-room while we were underway. I didn't expect to find trouble, merely wanting to see *Lionel*'s mechanical guts hard at work, but when I arrived below rivulets of fuel oil were running down the side of the port tank and spreading over the engine-room floor. This was not only messy but worrying. The workings of a diesel engine, then and to some extent still, are like foreign territory to me. And one of its mysterious features is that more fuel is pumped to it than it appears able to use. The excess is carried away by a pipe and dumped into one of the fuel tanks. It was this pipe that had come adrift. To fix it we had to moor the boat and the act of trying to stop the engine after mooring revealed the third and final problem of the day; the control to stop the engine refused to do so. By tracing the cable down to the engine I found, at last, the little lever that releases compression and brought everything to a stop. The fuel leak was easily fixed but the engine stop control, newly installed at St Cloud, turned out to be faulty and had to be replaced. That was a tiresome business in itself. For the rest of our trip to Auxerre and some time after, the only way to stop the engine was to go below and jiggle the little lever.

Shortly after these incidents we reached the Yonne River which rises in the hills of Morvan and flows north through Clamecy, Auxerre, Joigny and Sens, joining the Seine at Montereau, a place of some importance to commercial barges. Navigable up to Auxerre where it joins the Canal du Nivernais, the Yonne is a tranquil and quietly beautiful river meandering between overgrown banks through the farmland of Burgundy. But, for us, its attractions are counterbalanced by its amazingly long and notorious locks. Few people, including barge captains, speak well of them for clearly apparent reasons. Quite different from most French locks, many are constructed with sloping walls of rough stone instead of the normal vertical ones. These and the few steps provided for access to the lockside become slimy, making it extremely difficult to get ashore to secure a boat. When the water is being lowered in the lock these same walls also become a hazard on which a boat can easily become 'hung up'. It was only later that we started using the ladders on some of the gates which greatly simplified tying up in these wretched locks but going through them always remained an unpleasant experience not only because of their design but also because of the time it usually took and the lock-keepers themselves, seemingly a breed apart.

There are, of course, pleasant exceptions but for the most part the lock-keepers on the Yonne have always seemed a dour, silent and unhelpful lot if not, at times, downright sullen. We had experienced these locks before in a hire boat and were not looking forward to our first encounter with them in *Lionel*. Our docking in the first lock was a lamentable mess. As the lock-keeper stood impassively watching we put out a ramp along which Melodie scrambled to the slimy steps. Once on top of the sloping wall she seemed a long way off, the distance slowly increasing as *Lionel* drifted out. I then started throwing ropes, a skill at which I thought myself reasonably accomplished. But the distance was too great or the ropes too heavy for throw after throw failed to reach Melodie, landing instead on the slimy wall and sliding into the water, until she managed finally to put her foot on the tail of one before it too disappeared in the lock. Such a show of incompetence must have fixed for ever in the mind of the sour-faced, motionless lock-keeper his already healthy prejudice against all those who sail in pleasure boats.

Not long after this we were held up by some emergency repairs to a weir upstream. We moored for the night and remained tied up the following day. Other boats soon joined the line-up . . . four barges, one of them *Nelly*, and a gaggle of miscellaneous craft, tugs, flat-bed barges, a crane and two small yachts. We were off again the next morning with two travelling companions, a barge from Dunkerque loaded with soy-bean meal for animal feed and a home-made yacht. The three of us passed through the next few locks together. The barge captain was a nice and unusually talkative man who had no love of these locks or their keepers and made life a lot easier for us by allowing us to moor alongside his barge, instructing me carefully how it should be done with the propeller turning *doucement* (slowly) and the rudder at *moyen* (centred). He later came on board for a glass of wine and, like most barge people, was full of waterway stories. Born and brought up in Dunkerque he was eleven when the Germans arrived in the town and remembered them commandeering barges for the invasion of England. He recalled also the scepticism in the barge fraternity of the time about the probable fate of the barges in the kind of waves the Channel could produce. The long, flat-bottomed barges would, they thought, probably break up if conditions weren't ideal. They could have been right but we shall never know.

We also shared these same locks with a duo of late-middle-aged, charming but utterly disorganised Frenchmen in a boat one of them had designed and built himself. It was a strange craft, minuscule, top-heavy and under-powered. The crew was very new to boating, this being their maiden voyage. Needing all the help they could get, we allowed them to tie to our boat in the locks. We could thus examine their standard of seamanship at close hand. It wasn't very high but who were we to talk after the shameful episode in the first Yonne lock?

Their ropes were always in a mess, requiring a last minute scramble just before mooring and their knots, highly original in design, were nothing less than quixotic in performance, often unhitching themselves at critical moments rather the way Melodie's do. Because of the state of their ropes there was always understandable uncertainty about what was happening at each end of them and on more than one occasion a rope thrown to our boat was found, embarrassingly, not to be attached to theirs. But it was the wind that caused their boat most trouble and it suffered dreadfully in the near-gale that came up two days before reaching Auxerre. So much of the little boat was above water and so little below, it became all but uncontrollable, especially when forced to wait outside a lock. Once in the lock ourselves, we would gaze back with pity at our friends pirouetting helplessly outside, at last straightening out the boat enough to make a mad, crab-like dash for the haven of the lock.

Because the locks on the Yonne are very long, some of the lock-keepers have the lazy habit of opening only one gate for a boat of *Lionel*'s size so that they can avoid the long walk around to open the other one. It is a tight squeeze at the best of times and wind makes it very tricky, although one can sometimes accept this in the interest of speed. Late one afternoon, as we approached a lock, the gates were closed. We waited an unconscionable time with no action being taken, although the water was down and the lock-keeper only had to open one gate. I finally walked to the lock in the advancing dusk to find the lock-keeper trying to repair some lock mechanism with wire. In an attempt to help him, I suggested he open the other gate, but he greeted this with silence. I then said that, if he wished, we could moor for the night below the lock. In a foul temper, he shouted: 'No! You must go through the lock!' So we waited. The wind increased, night fell and at last we passed the lock. The lock-keeper airily indicated that bollards existed on the bank upstream but, if so, they certainly didn't show themselves, even after searching in the long grass with a flashlight, and we reluctantly tied the boat to mooring stakes, cherishing more unkind thoughts about the keepers of the Yonne River locks.

The wind that night and the following day was very strong, so strong, we later heard, that it blew the roof off a barge's wheelhouse in Auxerre. In a minor way we also suffered from it when we were blown into shallow water near the bank while waiting for a lock. *Lionel* is a heavy boat, difficult to push with a pole at any time and, against a wind, almost impossible. But we had to get free and Melodie, who hates doing this more than anything, did her best. When I thought the boat was out far enough I put it in gear, turning the propeller slowly. There was the kind of sound that clutches at a captain's vitals as the screw noisily began to re-arrange the rocks on the river bottom. In spite of the awful noise, I kept the screw turning and could only pray that the damage would be less severe than it sounded. Hoping for the best we completed our journey in the high wind, arriving during the late afternoon in the port of Auxerre where we would spend the winter.

Winter in Auxerre

Auxerre, or Ausserre as the natives say it, lies in the north-western corner of Burgundy eighty-seven miles south-east of Paris. It is an old town with a long history. Joan of Arc passed this way twice in 1429, the second time at the head of an army of 12,000 men to escort Charles VII to his coronation at Reims. And it was here that Napoléon, on his return from Elba, had that fateful meeting with Marshal Ney who had been sent to confront him but instead, enthusiastically put himself and his own army in the service of the Emperor. Now an important provincial town of 50,000 people, Auxerre still retains much of the urban fabric it has accrued over the centuries and is one of the best wintering ports on the waterways of France. Located outside the battlegrounds of both world wars, it has managed to escape the dreadful destruction that swept through so many of the older towns in the north and west. It rises magnificently at a bend in the River Yonne, old stone buildings encrusting the hill, packed tightly together in the random pattern of ancient cities. Threading through this dense matrix, the narrow streets, a few still cobbled, zig-zag their way to the top, making Auxerre a rewarding though demanding place for walking. From the opposite bank of the river the view is especially dramatic. The old city clambers up the hill to the summit dominated by the fifteenth-century cathedral of St Étienne, flanked on the south by l'Église St Pierre-en-Vallée and on the north by the old Abbaye St Germain. This trio of great churches creates an exciting skyline at the crown of the hill, and when they are floodlit at night the effect is stunning.

Not long after we arrived in Auxerre the Canal du Nivernais was closed, making the port the winter terminus of any traffic coming up the Yonne. The odd barge still came to deliver coal or load with grain but all the hire boats had been lifted out of the water and the port settled down for the winter. It was time to start rebuilding *Lionel*'s badly disordered insides. Art, the carpenter who would do this, was in

Auxerre and ready to start. Dutch by birth, an electronics technician by training, Art had lived in Canada for ten years when he worked at the government rocket range near Fort Churchill on Hudson Bay. He had become a Canadian citizen and then returned to Holland where he had since worked as a carpenter, mainly on boats and acquired for himself a beautiful old sailing barge which he lived on when in Amsterdam. He was to work on *Lionel* for half the winter and, during those weeks, became a friend.

From careful measurements in the boat I had, the previous summer, prepared detailed drawings of what was to be done. As an architect this came easily to me but boats are very different from buildings. In boats there is nothing that is, or should be assumed to be, plumb, level, rectangular or even straight. The boat designer must also think in much smaller dimensional increments than even in a small house because of the need to exploit every inch of limited space. The drawings I'd done would be useful as a guide but the boat itself would greatly influence the work and the process of rebuilding always remained a flexible one with changes being made along the way.

Much more had to be demolished before any new work could begin, revealing as it usually does, yet more problems to be solved and as the demolition advanced, the inside of the boat soon became a shambles. Bits of wood, fibre board, insulation, loose wiring and scattered tools littered the floor and a choking pall of dust filled the remaining space, making the boat quite uninhabitable. Help, however, was not far away.

Earlier, wandering down the quay, I had noticed a familiar barge, the *St Georges*, last seen several years ago in Sens when we had been in a hire boat. It then had two Americans aboard to whom we had talked briefly but I didn't recognise the woman I now saw working on deck. Assuming the barge had changed owners and was now French-owned, I struck up a conversation in schoolboy French. She responded in the same language and we pursued a faltering dialogue, each tactfully probing the background of the other. As this went back and forth for several minutes I became aware of something vaguely familiar about her. After a while it must have dawned on both of us about the same time that the other was hardly speaking French as a native would and we gratefully switched to English. It turned out she was indeed the person met before at Sens and was spending the winter alone on her boat in Auxerre. And it was Katharine, the warm and entertaining châtelaine of the *St Georges*, who, taking pity, gave us lodging on her boat for three weeks during the time of the worst upheaval in *Lionel*.

43

She became a good friend to us both, adding much needed flavour and extra spice to those long winter months in Auxerre.

The condition of our boat in those days greatly lowered my spirits. In the whole rehabilitation of *Lionel* it must have been the lowest point. Hardly a part of the interior was untouched by demolition and more bad news was being uncovered each day. It seemed like the last straw when the WC finally collapsed. But there could certainly be no turning back. I was more resolved than ever to push ahead and put the old barge once again into first-class shape. Of course, construction did, at last, replace destruction and slowly, oh so slowly, things began to improve.

I helped in the boat as much as I could but many hours had to be spent searching for the materials and equipment the renovation required. Although Art had his little Ford van for the larger things, all I had at the beginning was a bicycle borrowed from Katharine or later, one of our own. It was not the perfect vehicle for long distance winter travel and had gross deficiencies when used for haulage. But being all I had, it served nobly in its limited bicycle way, lugging all sorts of ungainly loads back to the boat from the distant suburbs of Auxerre, at times so heavily loaded I wondered if we would make it home at all. Long pieces of lumber strapped to the side were an especially troublesome load, seeming determined to restrict the bicycle exclusively

to straight-line travel and there were, at times, loads on the back so heavy they forced it into sudden and uncontrollable 'wheelies' at unexpected moments. When later bought, the Vespa Ciaio scooter gave a greater range of operations with less effort but was colder to ride and only marginally superior as a two-wheeled truck.

I suppose our most serious problem during that winter's work had to do with obtaining materials and equipment. This was partly due to the limited resources of Auxerre, a town of no great size, but more, I think, because France as a whole does not offer an extensive range of all the things needed for boats. This was a constant source of frustration and due to this limitation we were forced to work with the materials locally available rather than those of better quality. For anything more exotic than everyday lumber, plywood, hardware and tools one would have to search elsewhere, in a large city, possibly even Paris. And for any special boat equipment, it was certainly Paris, where one of the costly ship chandlers would gladly take one's order but was far from swift to deliver. And once the order finally arrived, one felt blessed if the right thing had been sent, had no bits missing and instructions were enclosed.

France has a well-earned reputation in Europe for going its own way regardless of the feelings and practices of neighbours or allies. It may be France's independent spirit or nothing more than chauvinistic bloody-mindedness but, whatever it's called, it exists and it was present even in the renovation of *Lionel*. When first met, it had to do with pipes. I would have thought that by now the countries of western Europe could have got together, at least on pipes, if for very little else, but it is not so. *Lionel* is a Dutch boat with Dutch pipes in the heating system. This system had to be modified and we soon found France has its own ideas about pipes. French pipe sizes are different from those in some other countries. There were no fittings available to make the conversion from one size to the other, so we were faced with two expensive options: every pipe connection would have to be brazed or welded at the joints or, equally drastic, all the pipes would have to be replaced. The latter proved quicker and probably cheaper but it was not to be the only time French self-assertiveness tripped us up in this way.

During that winter in Auxerre I also learnt something important about handling a barge, but the lesson came in a hard, humiliating way. *Lionel* had to be moved to a new mooring on the quay, a simple enough manoeuvre in prospect, but one which turned into a captain's nightmare. All I had to do was head downstream, turn and come back to the new mooring. It didn't seem excessively difficult although the river current had to be reckoned with, as well as wind, never a popular element with me. Melodie and Art were aboard as we went downstream under the *passerelle*. Just below the line of moored boats I tried to turn to starboard. This failed as both wind and current joined forces to thwart me, the boat refusing to come around. Starting then from the other side of the river, I tried again, to the port. But I was too close to the bank and, as the stern swung around, the wheelhouse, with much cracking and scraping, removed the lower branches from an overhanging tree. This attempt also failed. By that time the river had carried the boat into a wider section. This was good. But it was not good that we were now being carried inexorably towards a bridge with a weir beyond. Melodie and Art looked as worried as I felt. The third time, thank God, with more room to spare, I finally turned *Lionel* upstream in a wide, sweeping arc.

As is so often the case when making an exhibition of oneself, there was a large audience of interested spectators taking it all in from the shore and from the *passerelle*. Some of the latter, I noticed, were acquaintances from St Cloud. What cruel fate had brought them to this place, in this town, at this hour of this day to be witnesses of my humiliation?

As I approached our new mooring with the embarrassing tree branches littering the deck, I came in slowly but, having misjudged the current, not slowly enough. And as luck had it that day, there was a small plastic rowing-boat where we had to go. Just before *Lionel* snuffed out the little boat's life, its owner, standing nearby, plucked it smartly from the water. It was, alas, my misfortune on this unlucky day, that the owner was none other than the Taipan of the Port de Plaisance. Never a man to hold his tongue, he made sure I knew how little pleased he was.

It was all a very humbling experience out of which came two useful lessons. Lesson 1 should not have been necessary. It was an old one but in need of repetition: the 'golden rule' about always approaching a dock very, very slowly. Lesson 2 was about turning a barge and was new ground for me. Barges cannot be turned like small boats: they require a quite different technique, particularly when there is both wind and current to contend with. I owe this lesson to Art who filled so many gaps in my knowledge of barges and their operation. He explained that one must first stop the forward motion of the boat. Having done this the rudder is put hard over at about 60 degrees to the axis of the keel and the throttle pushed forward to near maximum power. It worked like a charm, the boat almost turning in its own length.

With winter came a need for heat. At the beginning all we had were little infra-red heaters mounted on top of fat butane bottles. Because this combination vaguely resembled the space being in a recent film these heaters were always referred to as ETs on *Lionel*. They gave good if costly heat but were a massive source of condensation and it was imperative that the central-heating system be put in operation. Since the radiators were all installed it only remained to start the furnace. This was an old-fashioned affair, similar to heaters used on many barges, consisting of a fire-box with water circulating in a coil of pipes above it. Oil simply dribbled in a more or less controlled flow on to a pan at the bottom of the fire-box and, when lit, heated the water in the pipes. Simple enough in theory; no moving parts, no sophisticated controls. After installing the chimney with its wonderful whirling bonnet on top I went below to tackle the furnace, a small steel box in the corner of the engine-room.

Finding the access door located for maximum inconvenience, as so many seem to be, I cleaned the fire-box in a half-hearted way and turned on the oil. When a little puddle of the stuff had collected I threw in a lighted piece of paper and the oil burst into feeble flame. The trick then was to let the oil burn for a while and adjust the flow until a clean blue flame appeared in the fire-box. I never quite achieved that mystic ideal but the strange little furnace worked after a fashion, though always fell short of supplying the required amount of heat. It was a great improvement over the ETs but fell far short of the modern furnace later installed.

About two weeks before Christmas warnings came from the Service de la Navigation to expect unusually high levels in the river, already swollen after several days of rain, its brown water curling angrily around the bridge piers. It seemed wise to take precautions. We were especially concerned that, with water high enough, the boat might be floated on to the quay and left there, high and dry. With Art's help steps were taken to forestall this. Two stout baulks of timber were lashed vertically to the quay side of the boat with their bottom ends on the river bed and their tops above the deck railings. These would prevent the boat floating on to the quay, but other measures were needed to hold the boat in place against the strong current. The new hundred-pound anchor was manhandled upstream along the quay, thrown into the water and the slack in the anchor chain taken up with the winch. Extra mooring lines were also rigged. During the flood these lines had to be checked periodically and adjusted to suit the rise and fall of water. If not done, the ropes might become taut as the water rose, finally tilting the boat and, if all else failed, would have to be cut.

The night when the flood began to rise was a restless one. Melodie and I were both up several times checking that all was well and at two-thirty I put another mooring line on the bow, the two already there stretched rigid by the force of the current. In the morning the water was over the quay, continuing to rise throughout the day. The same crew routine prevailed the following night as we did the rounds with a flashlight but, apart from abandoning ship, there was little more that we could do. By dawn the water had reached its maximum height, spreading fifteen to thirty yards inland over the quay, and effectively cutting us off from the land, except for Melodie who had equipped herself with some massive fisherman's hip waders reaching to the upper thigh. The ordinary folk were not so equipped and had to wait for the flood to subside and the boat to regain its normal relationship with the quay.

As the river slowly returned to a more normal level, the tempo of social life picked up in the port. Christmas was soon upon us and we celebrated this first in a kind of Anglo-Saxon *réveillon* on Christmas Eve with our daughter Caroline, Art and our new friends, Lynda and Johnny, late of British Airways, who had their own barge, the *Amity Belle*, moored nearby. Usually taking place late on Christmas Eve or New Year's Eve *réveillon* is the principal feast of the French at this time of year. We didn't follow the Gallic pattern exactly but it certainly was a feast. Melodie had bought for the occasion, at undisclosed cost, an entire giant cold poached salmon elaborately embellished in the elegant *haute cuisine* tradition. After dealing with that and all its delicious outriders we walked up through the dark, frosty streets for midnight mass in the great floodlit cathedral on the hill. About three hundred heavily clothed citizens of the town stood in a tightly packed group before the altar at one end of the frigid nave. Although there was a service it was an abbreviated one, giving way to Christmas music, both familiar and refreshingly new. An energetic woman whipped the small congregation into reluctant action, shepherding them through the carols with vigorous arm-waving. The combined result of voices, organ and a surprising single trumpet was certainly pleasant but there was an almost pathetic inadequacy about the whole event. I am not a church-going man but am familiar with the Roman Catholic Mass as it used to be and, as a non-involved spectator, valued it for its pageantry, especially against the background of beautiful old churches. I liked the dim, candle-lit chancels, the sparkling, elaborately garnished altars. I liked the rich, heavy vestments of the priests and the way they silently went about their mysterious business. I liked the music, the processions, the use of Latin, even the incense. Perhaps I liked these things for the wrong reasons, having nothing to do with the Mass myself, but I enjoyed its theatre and its mystery and its rightness for its surroundings. Most of this has, alas, been swept away. What remains has little drama and certainly no mystery. It is laid bare and ordinary. Standing there in the icy nave of St Étienne as we sang our carols, I looked around at the ancient stones and thought to myself that they demanded more than this.

In early January, the port suddenly became busier. First to arrive was a Belgian barge going upstream through the Pont Paul Bert to take on a load of grain at the storage elevators. A little later the barge ran aground on a mud bank and slewed around in the strong current to finish across an arch of the old bridge. It was a tricky situation as the water of the swollen river piled up against the massive side of the barge, tilting it alarmingly. The young captain in the stern appeared calmer than the situation might have warranted but the woman in the bow, later discovered to be his sister, had already prepared for the worst and donned a life-jacket. They remained in this awkward predicament for several hours as ineffectual efforts were made by the *sapeurs-pompiers* to pull the barge free. The firemen, who in France also deal with water emergencies, finally succeeded and the Belgians moored on the quay near us. The young crew had been through a bad time so we took them a bottle of whisky to cheer them up. I doubt, however, that it did much to wipe out the memory of Auxerre. Not only had the captain got into grave trouble above the bridge, but he had damaged his wheelhouse going through it and, we heard later, also smacked the bow of his barge on the lock wall as he was leaving the port.

The renewed coming and going of barges injected something strong and vital into the port's sleepy winter existence. For us it was important to have contact again, however casual, with the men and women who operate the working barges of the French canals. The barges are the very essence of the inland waterways, the reason they are there. They bring to the canals and rivers the hard realities of the commercial world and the hard realities of their crews' own working lives. It cannot be an easy life: scratching a bare living from work days that stretch from dawn to dusk and raising families in the confined quarters of their boats. But the rivers and canals are enriched by these people, by the lore and traditions of their work and the high level of professional skill they bring to it.

Art's allotted time in Auxerre at last came to an end and in mid-January he returned to Holland. He had worked long, hard and well to do far more than any of us expected. The major carpentry and cabinet work were done but much still remained. Although not complicated, the task seemed formidable in prospect as I faced it alone. It was repetitive and fiddly work involving all the door frames, ceiling battens and wood trim throughout the boat, each piece having to be measured, cut, fitted, drilled, sanded and installed. It took three months of steady work and I was very thankful when it finally came to an end in March. But at least the results of so much labour were beginning to show. The cabinet work was 90 per cent complete, the heating system was working, albeit feebly, the generator problems were sorted out (for the time being) and its new fuel tank installed. Painting and varnishing were well underway as was the making of curtains and cushion covers by Melodie. When I returned to *Lionel* after a short trip to Canada it looked at last like a place where two people and a Dalmatian could live in some comfort.

Spring came to Auxerre in March, bringing warm, sunny days and tiny, bright green leaves to the riverside trees. After the long winter with the barge moored to the quay, thoughts of moving again began to stir the mind. So we set off on a short cruise down the Canal du Nivernais to the south with our friend Katharine who would leave after a day or so and ride back on her bicycle. We spent the first night at Vermenton at the end of a short branch canal. It is a small, out-of-the-way village on the little River Cure which flows through the mooring basin and the beautiful little park that is Vermenton's special pleasure, narrow rivulets of the Cure winding their way among the trees and over diminutive waterfalls. The gentle plopping of these, the distant cries of children playing, and the soft 'chunk' of *boules* landing on the gravel courts are the only sounds in this peaceful spot where I never tire of spending time.

The following day at Mailly la Ville we returned to *Lionel* at dusk to find the sky full of migrating starlings, a flock far larger than either of us had ever seen before. There must have been thousands of them wheeling in the sky, a shifting pattern of grey and black as they swerved this way and that just above our heads, seeking places to roost for the night. Flowing in great waves over the canal in the half-light, groups would separate and come together again in an ever-changing aerial pattern, sometimes suddenly dropping to the trees like small tornadoes. The visual impact of the constant fluid motion was as staggering as the whirring sound of all those fluttering wings in the still evening air.

The winter was over now and shortly after our return to Auxerre we had to fly home to Canada. Arrangements were made to moor *Lionel* beside the barge belonging to Alan, another friend, who would be living on his boat during the summer, giving *Lionel* the best kind of security. The bills were paid and the boat prepared for the untenanted months ahead, always an unhappy task, a bit like closing up a house that one has come to love. Then the farewells were said to all our newly made friends and we drove out of the Port de Plaisance past Katharine, standing by her boat in a huge, old straw hat, sadly waving the small Canadian flag we'd given her. Then reluctantly to the north and the little hotel in the country that has become for us a much needed quiet interval before and after the hurly-burly of the airport.

Auxerre *encore*

In September 1983 Joss and I returned to France alone, Melodie planning to join us about a month later. At the airport, handling Joss, her cage and all the baggage was never easy. Single-handed, it felt like a doomed amateur balancing-act as I pushed the tottering cart across the floor towards *les douanes* with Joss pulling awkwardly at her leash. We sailed through all the barriers, no one seeming to care about either of us or even bothering to look at Joss's carefully assembled health credentials. It has always been this way with Joss and I suppose if one wanted to import a really rabid dog into France, Paris airport might be a pretty safe bet. Be that as it may, we trundled on to the car rental desk and, after that, to the lift up to the cars overhead. As the doors opened, I pushed the heavily loaded cart forward. Its front wheels caught on the sill, dumping all the bags and the bits of Joss's disassembled cage at the feet of a surprised man standing at the back of the lift. As he stood coolly watching me, I hastily put the scattered bags and cage back on the cart and, a little flustered, withdrew, after discovering it was the wrong lift after all.

Back again in the Port de Plaisance I found *Lionel* dirtier but otherwise none the worse for our summer's absence and I set about getting it ready for occupancy. Much needed to be done but Melodie was not due to join me for a month and, being alone with few distractions or diversions, I could buckle down to work long hours each day, hoping to have accomplished great things by the time she arrived. But before starting work I went looking for a car.

It was time to add this luxury to our life in France for bicycles, even a scooter, are one person vehicles and give one too small a radius of operation beyond the boat. We had been missing much because of this. With a car we could explore further afield, perhaps visit countries other than France as well. While moving on the boat we could, of course, carry the car with us as many commercial barges do or simply return by train to pick it up when needed. The latter alternative seemed preferable. Carrying a car on deck poses problems like getting it on and off but these are minor compared with the penalty of having to look over the top of a car as one floats through France. And, we later found, the train trip to pick up the car was often an enjoyable break away from the boat.

Finding and buying the car itself was, as might be expected, a fairly predictable series of events. There was, of course, an unbridgeable gulf between the car I'd set my heart on and the price I was prepared to pay. After making compromises in both areas and an exhaustive search of the used car lots, I finally settled, almost in desperation, on a bright red Renault 5. The price seemed too high. I offered to buy at a lower one. The dealer wouldn't budge and I knew I was licked. I gave the car a cursory look, took it for a test drive and bought it. I regretted the purchase ever after, the car turning out to be badly designed, difficult to drive and so consumed with rust that we later feared rear seat passengers might slip silently through the floor. But it had four wheels and it worked in a rough and ready kind of way. To the day we parted, it doggedly and noisily did what was asked of it.

After all the business with cars I soon got down to serious work on *Lionel*. During the summer twelve new windows had arrived for the boat from England to replace the old fixed ones and I set about the long, boring job of installing them. Twenty-six holes had to be drilled through the quarter-inch steel superstructure for each one, then the window fastened with twenty-six stainless steel self-tapping screws and each of these cut off with a cold chisel because they were too long. After doing each of these operations three hundred and twelve times, I had had enough and was glad to get back to carpentry, the fine weather allowing me to work most of the time on deck, with Joss lying nearby, her spots gradually disappearing under a fine layer of wood shavings and sawdust. It was a time of major change for *Lionel*. I was able to finish the kitchen cupboards and lay its new cork floor. Carpet was laid by others throughout the main living areas of the boat and, with insulation, was applied to the steel upper part of the outside walls to stop the condensation which had been such a problem the previous winter.

One of the minor and, as I thought in prospect, more enjoyable little tasks undertaken that autumn in Auxerre was the installation of the newly arrived compressed air horn, a powerful affair with a reputed carrying distance of a mile. It came with all its parts but no instructions or wiring diagram. Having obtained help for the latter from a friend I began to install the various bits and pieces, almost immediately dropping the relay, a small but vital part, behind the instrument panel in the wheelhouse. I heard it bounce down into a dark, narrow crevice below, making intriguing little noises as it hit this and that en route to what I felt would be certain oblivion. Knowing how long it had taken to get this horn and how long it would take again to replace the relay, I was despondent. With a flashlight I could see the little thing faintly at the bottom of what was a thin eight-foot-deep shaft, the kitchen wall on one side and the steel engine-room bulkhead on the other. There was no access whatever but I thought if I could see it there must be a chance of recovery. Using the powerful magnet we had for recovering tools dropped in the water, I lowered this on a string hoping to grab the lost relay. But the magnet was drawn inexorably to the steel bulkhead, clinging there tenaciously and couldn't be persuaded to reach the bottom where it was meant to do its work. There remained only one other thing I could do. Having paid heavily for the wood panelling in the kitchen I was understandably reluctant to cut holes in it but it seemed the only way. And this I did, after making careful measurements, to find the relay right behind the hole I'd cut. In triumph I returned to the job of installation, this time carefully securing the relay on a little leash of string.

Living alone meant that I worked long hours, breaking off tired in the late afternoon for the reward of a few drinks sitting in the wheelhouse with Joss. The meal that followed came mostly from a frying-pan, the lazy man's unhealthy solution to cooking when alone. I never much enjoy cooking for myself and resort more than I should to the simple and quick which also simplifies the washing-up. Fortunately for most of the time I was by myself, two good friends, Sylvia and Gordon, were on his barge next door to *Lionel*. On many evenings I joined them on their deck sipping rum and orange-juice as the sun set behind the cathedral on the hill across the river. It was the best time of the day and, after long hours of dusty toil, I always looked forward to these times on the deck of the *Neeltje* as the three of us sipped our drinks in the fading light.

It was during those autumn months that *Lionel* acquired a new furnace and a new hot-water heater, both installed by Jeremy, a young Englishman, who had already done much work on our boat. It was the second, smaller piece of equipment that concerned me most since it was going into a part of the boat that had already been finished, with easily damageable surfaces everywhere. The hard experience of the last month warned me to expect complications and there were. The chimney of the new hot-water heater was larger than the old one, requiring a larger hole through the ceiling and steel superstructure with all the disorder, mess and undoing of earlier work this would entail. I was not thrilled by the prospect. Jeremy's presence in the boat would also introduce again the instant chaos that plumbers seem to have a talent for and so it proved. The inside of *Lionel* soon began to resemble the state it had been in before reconstruction started. Ceiling panels and insulation lay casually about, the plumbing had been disconnected and every square foot of the kitchen, the deck outside the wheelhouse, even part of the quay was covered with pipes, wires, tools and odd bits of equipment. It was a constant source of wonder to me that one man, engaged on what was a fairly minor operation, could have such a marked and widespread influence on the local environment. Are plumbers all like this? I'm not sure but I was absolutely certain that in the coming chaotic frenzy more could be laid to waste and much damage done if things were allowed to get out of hand.

That fear came into sharp focus when the hole in the steel roof had to be enlarged with a cutting torch. As a welder myself I knew the hazards of this operation which could set molten metal dancing about the kitchen. To prevent this during the cutting operation, I held up to the hole a tray filled with damp sand and stones. It worked, up to a point, collecting the molten metal and most, but not all, the sparks. Those that escaped around my head went on their merry way and I could do nothing to stop them. Once the cutting was finished I discovered that the tray held above my head was plastic and not metal as I had thought. I am lucky, I suppose, that the torch didn't burn right through it with distressing consequences for my scalp immediately below.

With our departure for the south of France impending, it still remained to solve the problem of the anchor chain. *Lionel* now had a reasonable anchor and a proper barge winch had been installed during the summer, but the links in the chain already on the boat were too small to mesh with the 'gypsy' on the winch, a special cog-wheel over which the chain passes and holds it securely when the anchor is being used. I had no wish to venture on the big rivers to the south without a working anchor, so a chain had to be found before we left. I had searched high and low for one without success as had others on my behalf. When our departure drew closer and a solution became more urgent I was forced, finally, to consider buying new chain . . . a costly way to go. Such chain was available from Paris at 100 francs a metre, the required forty metres, value added tax of 18.6 per cent and shipping bringing the total close to 5,000 francs. It was not an attractive prospect but I was desperate and placed the order.

As so often happens, right after doing this, a friend reported seeing used chain of the same size in a boatyard not far away at Montereau. I phoned the boatyard immediately and spoke to the *patron*. He said: 'Yes, I have eighty to a hundred metres of chain your size'. I asked him the price for forty metres. '60,000 francs', he replied. There was a long pause at my end of the line. He must have found my silence strange for he said: 'Do you find that expensive?' I was on the point of saying something in French like: 'You're damned right,' when the little wheels started to whir and click into place as I recalled the quaint reluctance of the French to part with the 'old franc', long since abandoned officially but still used by older French citizens in business dealings. The *patron* then confirmed that he had, indeed, given me the price in 'old francs'. Since I didn't know then the relationship between 'old' and 'new' franc I asked for the price in the latter. This came over the telephone from Montereau as 600 francs, a very reasonable price, and I relaxed with relief. I now had two chain options; a new one for about 5,000 francs and a used one, but functionally the same, for 600 francs. I tried to cancel the order for the former but was too late. An arrangement was, however, made with the Paris company who agreed to the cancellation in return for a penalty payment of 300 francs. I paid this gladly and was then free to buy the second-hand chain, resulting in a saving of almost 4,500 francs, a most unusual outcome for me.

Melodie, at last, returned to France at the end of October, a month later than expected because of a boating expedition of her own up the Amazon. She arrived at a time when the hotels of Paris are often jammed with visitors to one of the annual Salons like the motor or *Prêt à Porter* (ready-to-wear) shows. The only hotel I could find within taxi distance of the airport with a room to spare and a relaxed attitude towards dogs was an awful place in the equally awful suburb of Pantin. Here I met Melodie who found my choice of hotel a little odd but didn't complain and the following morning we set off for Auxerre, stopping first in another suburb of Paris to load our new dinghy on to the roof of the car and then on to Montereau to pick up the anchor chain. At the boatyard, the chain was already laid out on the grass for us but after one look at the heavily loaded little Renault, with the dinghy tied to the roof with bits of string, the boatyard people wisely dissuaded me from further challenging its already over-strained springs and we left the chain there.

The anchor chain was later retrieved from Montereau with the help of Johnny, a good friend, always generous with his time. After much struggling it was manhandled on to *Lionel*'s deck where no time was lost checking its fit to the 'gypsy'. Although the links had the required dimensions given to me earlier, I found to my horror that they did not mesh with the 'gypsy'. This was serious but I felt lucky, at least, that it wasn't the expensive new chain, with presumably the same link size, which now lay useless on the deck. All I could hope for now was that, on our way south, at the same boatyard, I could exchange this chain for one that worked. It would be the last chance.

Southward bound

Away finally at the end of October, we headed north down the Yonne. Because of our late departure only one route south now remained to us. The Canal du Nivernais would shortly be closed for the winter and the Canal de Bourgogne was blocked by a *chômage* (temporary closing for repairs). After reaching the Seine, therefore, we would turn south at St Mammès to follow the linked canals that eventually meet the Saône at Chalon. We left Auxerre behind with some regrets but were elated at being on the move again, the voyage south promising new adventures and a refreshing change of scene. Both *Lionel* and its crew would greatly benefit from the more active existence that lay ahead.

For the first part of our journey we enjoyed the luxury of a third working crew member. Lynda, whose husband was away in England, was a bonus from several points of view. It was good to have her aboard both for her own delightful self but also for her experience on barges. Having spent many years under her husband's stern captaincy she knew exactly where to be, what to do and when to do it. Lynda was also a fantastic jumper. Melodie learnt much from her and lost some of her own fear of jumping from the boat by watching the flying leaps of this younger addition to the crew. More than anything, having two able deck hands made the business of mooring and locking through a matter of effortless simplicity, even the horrendous Yonne locks seeming to have lost their menace. It was such a change from the normal case with only two of us aboard when much of the hard work falls to Melodie and, being at the wheel, there is little I can do to help.

During the first weeks after leaving Auxerre we were blessed with impeccable autumn weather. Warm, sunny, windless days followed each other in a long parade as we cruised down the Yonne in easy stages, stopping overnight at Joigny and spending *Toussaints* (All Saints' Day) at Sens, there visiting again the twelfth-century cathedral of St Étienne, the first great Gothic cathedral built in France and a strong influence on William of Sens who later reconstructed the choir of Canterbury Cathedral. We topped off the day in the bar of the Hôtel Paris et Poste with several gigantic Kirs, the aperitif of blended cassis and cold white wine so favoured in Burgundy, and an excellent meal of *moules farcies* and roast quail in a restaurant in the cathedral square. The following day on the Seine we moored at the 'anchor chain' boatyard just downstream from the special railway bridge carrying the TGV, France's fastest passenger trains, as they hurtled north or south. It was a tranquil mooring if you didn't mind your tranquillity coming in small packages separated by moments of wild, swishing racket made by the TGV as it sped by on its urgent business seventeen times a day.

Now the moment of truth had truly arrived, the last chance to sort out the bothersome problem of the anchor chain before we entered waters where an efficient winch/chain/anchor combination might make the difference between safety and shipwreck. We had moored alongside a derelict barge on which there was a pile of chains with different link sizes. Trying the most likely one on the 'gypsy', it seemed looser in the link-sized depressions than I could have wished but I judged it would do the job of paying out the chain and holding it fast with the winch brake on. But to be sure I asked the *patron* for his opinion. He was a heavy, stout man with glasses, a hat, and a thick, dark moustache. Clambering awkwardly up a narrow ramp and across the old barge he finally landed heavily on our deck. Crouching for some time beside the winch, he examined it and fiddled with the chain on the 'gypsy' before straightening up and saying: '*Ce n'est pas bon. Il y a trop de jeu*'.

It was a depressing judgment. There certainly was some '*jeu*' or play but I wouldn't have said too much. He must later have agreed or feared to lose the sale for, after taking a few measurements, he changed his mind and conveyed the comforting news that, in spite of the play, the chain would not slip out of the 'gypsy'. This was the essential requirement. The *patron* then gave us a little talk on chains, explaining that, in France, the links come in 10mm increments, their lengths being 75mm, 85mm, 95mm and so on. As one might have guessed, and quite inexplicably, the 'gypsy' of *Lionel*'s winch was made for links between 95mm and 105mm long! But the chain worked well enough, so we marked it off with coloured tape at five-yard intervals to show how much chain was in the water with the anchor down and transferred it to the boat.

Feeling much more secure in the anchor department we travelled the short distance down the Seine to St Mammès, the barge town at the junction with the Canal du Loing. Some years before we had been there at the time of a barge wedding, all the clustered barges decked out with fluttering flags and horns blaring, the bride and groom later walking solemnly along the quay at the head of a long procession of *marinier* families all dressed in their very best clothes. But this time it was business as usual when we took on more fuel for the journey south and turned into the Canal du Loing.

This canal, first built in the eighteenth century, is the most northerly of a series of canals linking the Seine to the Saône at Chalon and is, for me, the most attractive in the chain. It threads its way through an intimate, long-settled landscape of farmland and forest dotted with interesting small towns. Of these, the first and perhaps best, is Moret sur Loing, not far from Fontainebleau: a place of royal residence in the Middle Ages and still retaining fortifications from that period. More recently, the Impressionist painter, Sisley, spent the last twenty years of his life in Moret, dying there in poverty at the end of the last century. Clemenceau, the great French politician, also lived there for a while and it was opposite his old thatched cottage near the canal that we tied up for the night.

No bollards being available, we were forced to moor to stakes driven into the canal bank. These were not normal mooring pins but special stakes I'd made, based on the principle of the anchor. This was their first time in use and it remained to be seen whether they would stand up to the ultimate test posed by a passing loaded barge. Because it displaces a lot of water and canals tend to be narrow, the passage of such a barge creates peculiar and sometimes violent effects. It is like a large hole moving down the canal with water constantly rushing in to fill it, causing short-lived but severe currents which can do strange things to a moored boat, making it surge vigorously this way and that, and putting a great strain on the mooring arrangements.

At Moret, my confidence in the new stakes was still unshaken, until early in the morning I awoke to my early rising wife's near-hysterical shouts from the deck above my head, the high-pitched 'Hart!' sounding like a coot in great distress. When I scrambled up there she reported that the strain on the stern line had been so great as a barge passed that the stake had been ripped from the ground with an accompanying shower of sparks and flung into the water (later recovered with our powerful magnet.) It is doubtful if many stakes could have resisted such a force in the poor ground of the canal bank but later I made some with far greater holding power. As far as possible, however, we tried to avoid their use except in direst need, especially in narrow canals used by barges, always preferring to tie to bollards or trees, sometimes even on the towpath side by rigging the mooring lines high overhead to tree branches, thereby hoping to avoid decapitating unwary nocturnal cyclists.

The benign weather stayed with us all the way down the Loing. We stopped for a picnic lunch in the warm sun beside the canal, sitting on the dry autumn leaves with our backs against giant tree trunks, nibbling a simple pasta and salad which had never tasted so good before. Lazily we meandered on, the trees slipping by in the hazy autumn light until finally, at a lock in Nemours, we were met by Lynda's husband Johnny who, on his way back from England, had spent six hours searching for us on the canal. It is not difficult to understand and it can be a drawn-out, tiring business. Because one can't always drive along the towpath or even a road close to the canal, one must search for remote country locks over small back roads, ask the lock-keeper if the boat one is seeking has passed the lock and then trundle off to the next one. In this hide-and-seek game a boat can easily slip by unnoticed and the search goes on. By the time Johnny found us he was exhausted, badly in need of strong drink, food and sleep. He had all three aboard *Lionel* and left the next morning with Lynda.

The Loing is a pleasant, quiet, intimate canal with beautiful scenery, easy locks and nice lock-keepers. It also carries a surprising volume of commercial traffic. We enjoyed the presence of working *péniches* but on a narrow canal like the Loing they can create problems for other boats. The loaded *péniche* draws a lot of water, its flat bottom being very close to, if not actually scraping the canal bed, particularly on the Loing which is not a deep canal. A heavily laden barge in this situation cannot deviate much from the centre of the canal without striking the sloping sides. This condition sometimes serves as a kind of automatic pilot for the barge captain, the sloping bottom at the sides of the canal always returning the barge to the centre if it wanders off course. A friend reports passing such a barge once with no one in the wheelhouse, finding the experience both alarming and eerie. Shallow canals like the Loing are a problem for barge captains who naturally wish to carry the maximum load. In an effort to provide as much draft as possible the water levels are kept high, sometimes beyond the bounds of safety and have resulted in grave accidents. Some years ago, on the Canal de Briare south of the Loing, high-water levels caused a breach in the canal bank, sluicing a barge loaded with salt out of the canal and precipitating it into the Loire River valley far below.

When passing loaded barges, one encounters, once again, the 'moving hole in the water' phenomenon but, because both boats are in motion, the effect is different from that when moored. Although present as before, the rush of water back and forth is not so noticeable. It is the sudden lowering of the water level that one must be prepared for. In a narrow canal with a loaded barge occupying most of the main channel, there is not much room left and it is in the narrow space between the moving barge and the shallow water of the canal verge that one must manoeuvre one's boat as best one can, between the Scylla of collision on one side and the Charybdis of grounding on the other. As the boats pass, the water is first raised by the swell in front of the barge's blunt bow and then dramatically lowered as the two boats come abreast. I learned from hard experience on the Loing that such meetings should not be taken lightly. On more than one occasion *Lionel*'s turning screw struck rock, once so decisively that the engine was stopped cold. It seemed desirable to avoid this at all costs so I developed a routine to deal with these meetings. To maintain steerage way I kept the screw turning until bow was abreast of bow. I then put the engine out of gear, steering with the boat's momentum until the stern of the barge was past when it was safe again for the propeller to turn.

The Canal du Loing comes to an end about thirty miles south of the Seine near Montargis where it joins the Canal de Briare, the oldest canal in France, completed in 1642 but, unlike the Canal du Midi in the south, no longer possessing its original canal structures. Like the Loing, the Briare threads its way through rolling farm country of small fields and woodlands interrupted periodically by the attractive little towns dating from the canal's early days. Like most canals it had its own special personality composed of lock-keepers, locks and their machinery. Some of the last, sinuously curved cast-iron pedestals used for operating the upstream gates, acquired a bizarre second life at certain moments, turning themselves into impromptu and erratic little *jets d'eau*, squirting water under pressure in all directions out of their many cracks and orifices . . . amusing diversions best admired from a distance.

And many of the locks were unusually deep, requiring me often to throw ropes fifteen feet or more up to Melodie standing on the lockside above. With the new, heavier ropes and the older, weaker me, this was approaching my limit, but Melodie usually managed to snatch, or stamp on, the tail of the rope in the nick of time. As always, she performed magnificently: leaping from the boat into the often prickly, sometimes stinging and usually hidden hazards of the canal bank, climbing high, slimy steel ladders in the locks, tying ropes with her unique but surprisingly effective knot, closing and opening stubborn lock gates and always finding time for cheery chats with lock-keepers.

The Canal de Briare comes to an end at the town of Briare where the great nineteenth-century aqueduct designed by Eiffel carries the canal over the Loire River after which it becomes the Canal Latéral à la Loire to continue further south. This must be the finest canal aqueduct in France, perhaps Europe, over 700 yards long, with a row of light standards marching down both sides and embellished at each end with the kind of heavy romantic sculpture so loved by the French; altogether a remarkable bit of decorative engineering on an otherwise workaday canal. The Canal Latéral à la Loire goes south from here through country which seems flatter and less varied than that to the north. Although running beside the Loire for most of its length, the well-known château country is not to be found here but in a valley of the river running west from Briare. Good moorings were not easy to find, so we didn't linger but continued south, arriving at the end of a long day's cruise in Marseilles les Aubigny. There being no mooring below the lock, Melodie went in search of the lock-keeper whose young son finally helped her work the lock as we passed through into the basin beyond. It was by then pitch dark. I couldn't see where to moor or even where the shore was, but Melodie finally lit the way in with a flashlight.

Our mooring in the basin was against a stone wall across a road from the few shops serving this tiny village. Below these and perhaps a hundred yards away, the Loire flowed serenely south between sandy banks and willow clumps. In the basin, there was little activity, only the occasional barge passing through and a few signs of life aboard the seven moored barges sitting out the winter on the opposite side. It was a peaceful, if somewhat bleak, place where we were to stay for several days until Jeremy came from Auxerre to install some new equipment. As events unfolded, our stay in the area was to be a great deal longer than we could have guessed.

The following day was 11th November, Armistice Day. There was the usual ceremony at the local war memorial down the road but, two days later, something else was going on there. Curiosity aroused, we went to have a look. A group of men paraded down the village street wearing medals and carrying flags to the accompaniment of a loud and enthusiastic band of uniformed boys. Once the men had gathered around the memorial, a long roll call of people killed in the war was read, each name followed by an intoned: *Mort pour la France.* Meanwhile we saw another, smaller group crossing the canal bridge having just left a church on the far side where they had held, presumably, their own service of remembrance. But why was this happening on 13th November and why were there two groups? Making contact with the smaller group, we discovered they were the local branch of Resistance fighters calling themselves 'les Francs-Tireurs Partisans Français'. It was their group, they claimed, which had really done the fighting and the sabotage; they scorned the others at the war memorial as nothing more than non-combatants. They didn't want anything to do with them and it was for this reason that the smaller group always had a separate service on 13th November, the memorial day of the Resistance in France. Not content with only two groups of Resistance veterans, we were told France has even more, each, I suppose, saying unkind things about all the rest.

Our new acquaintances were wandering slowly in the direction of the local café to have a warming nip before their midday meal and asked us to join them. We all piled into the one tiny room of what may well be the smallest café in the whole of France. It had a bar to one side, walls and ceiling plastered with wild, highly coloured wallpaper, the pattern interrupted here and there by faded photographs of aged, moustached faces wearing hats and bleary looks. A beaten-up bar soccer game, a few rough wooden tables and chairs occupied most of the remaining space. The little room would have seemed crowded with ten but was now jammed with thirty or more women and cap-wearing men all crushed together in one jolly, chattering mass. Threading through this tightly packed, shifting jumble of bodies was the extraordinary figure of *la patronne* with her tray of drinks; a strange sight at any time but doubly so among these simple country folk. Dressed entirely in black from head to foot: black shoes, tight black slacks, studded black leather belt, black blouse hugging amazingly generous breasts, dyed jet-black hair, all coming to a startling climax in her creased middle-aged face encased in layers of gaudy make-up. This painted biker's moll weaved around among the farmers and their wives dispensing drinks and smiles as room was made for us at a table where we were given wine. We chatted away within the limits of our French and the prevailing din, our own war service providing a kind of common ground between us. They gave us their pins and we replied with cigars and small Canadian flags hastily brought from the boat. They were warm-hearted souls but we felt it best to leave them to their annual party and, at last, returned to *Lionel.* It was the brightest moment of our short stay in their village which was in every other way to be clouded by mechanical disaster.

Breakdown

Next day the blow fell. At Marseilles les Aubigny there was no shore power. Consequently, the batteries had to be charged regularly with the new generator we had installed when we were at St Cloud. Although it was then about a year old, it had not had a hard life aboard *Lionel*, having only been run for twenty hours because of the shore power available at Auxerre and there being no need of it when the boat was moving, the batteries then being charged by the main engine. But at Marseilles les Aubigny I was running the generator frequently, and depending heavily on it. Then in the late afternoon of that fateful day, hearing a sudden and marked change in the note of the generator's single-cylinder diesel motor, I knew that something untoward had taken place. I rushed to the wheelhouse where the relevant gauges and lights confirmed a death of sorts down below and I immediately shut the whole thing down.

It was then 15th November. Checking my files, I saw that the one-year guarantee had expired on 7th November, only eight days before! Somewhat stunned by this, I put in train the recovery operations without which we'd be in serious trouble. An electrician, kindly lent by the local hire-boat company, could only confirm that the trouble, whatever it was, lay inside the generator and beyond his skills to repair. But Jeremy in Auxerre, when told of our plight, arranged to come in a few days, bringing a portable generator to tide us over the crisis. In the meantime our only power was draining away as the tired old batteries slowly went downhill. We were reading with flashlights, using candles for general illumination and heating only with the ETs. It had become very cold by the time we reached electrical bottom when the batteries failed even to turn over the main engine. They were not only flat but at the end of their useful lives. With the arrival of Jeremy from Auxerre, bringing a portable generator and two enormous new batteries, morale aboard *Lionel* rapidly improved.

While Jeremy and I were installing the new batteries, Melodie suddenly appeared to report a new, minor but vexing problem quite unrelated to electricity. It appeared that the normally reliable Lavac WC was refusing to work. Compared to everything else, this seemed trifling but I abandoned what I was doing and went below. After disconnecting pipes to investigate all the likeliest points of blockage and finding none, I checked the translucent water intake pipe with a flashlight finding only a faint grey smudge at its connection to the bowl. Leaving Melodie to do some research on that, I returned to the engine-room. A few minutes later she appeared with a jar of water containing the cause of the trouble, the smallest catfish I have ever seen, still alive in spite of its awful ordeal, jammed in the pipe under great pressure. It must certainly have been gravely damaged but gamely swam away from the boat when released.

Because of the impending repairs to the generator, we moved *Lionel* along the canal to Nevers where the needed technical resources might be found. We also retrieved our car from Auxerre to make more enjoyable what could turn out to be a longish stay. Although not exceptional, Nevers is a pleasant enough provincial town with a good cathedral of mixed ancestry, a ducal palace, a long tradition of *faïence* production and the tomb of Bernadette whose visions started the long history of pilgrimage to Lourdes, currently reaching an astonishing figure of roughly five million people each year. She was canonised in 1933, and her preserved body now lies in the Couvent St Gildard where it has become one of the local tourist attractions.

Nevers is separated from the canal by the valley of the Loire, the nearest mooring being in the old commercial port at the end of a short branch canal which at one time was connected to the river. The basin of the old port should have been, but was not, a nice mooring when we knew it. It was certainly quiet but not much more. At one end, any possible view of the town was blocked by a decrepit factory building. The side of *Lionel*'s mooring was disfigured by abandoned warehouses with blank grey walls, one thirty feet from *Lionel* decorated with giant-sized, anatomically explicit pornographic graffiti. On the other side of the basin a ragged encampment of gypsies lived a hard and untidy existence in and around their modern trailers. As with such nomadic groups, their life was never clean or neat but had considerable interest for us. Sanitation was as basic as it can get, free use being made of the local ground by children and adults alike. The canal served as a garbage dump, a place for rare ablutions and as a source of water for washing clothes, dishes and for cooking. There always seemed to be great pots with unknown contents bubbling away over wood fires tended by the women who worked hard from dawn to dusk at washing, cooking and cleaning their cramped living quarters. The children played all day, never appearing to go to school and, like the children, the men stayed in the camp most of the time, never working or helping the women, just standing around the fires chatting. It was hard to see where the money came from to support even this simple way of life. Their big trailers and cars were neither cheap to buy nor run and, like everyone, they had to have food and supplies of every kind. There were many unanswered questions as we studied the daily lives of these people through binoculars. And they perhaps had some questions of their own as they watched us across the intervening water where ice was slowly forming as winter approached.

A man supposedly able to deal with our moribund generator at last arrived at the boat. I explained the problem to Monsieur Tissot who immediately started work. This continued for days in fits and starts, with problems followed by solutions rapidly followed by more problems, through bad moments and good, stretching well into December. It was a long and grisly story, involving the manufacturers, their agents, the installer and, inevitably, a lawyer, but I knew from the start that I would finish on the losing side and so it turned out many weeks later. The immediate need, however, was to find the cause of the breakdown and this Tissot managed to do after several hours' labour in the engine-room. He reported the grim news that the cast aluminium supports of the stator or fixed part of the generator had cracked in two places, causing the moving part, the rotor, to rotate itself eccentrically to death in one terminal paroxysm. The generator was finished, kaput, irreparable. The whole thing, except the diesel motor, had to be replaced and, since all the other parties involved were now nicely off the hook with an expired guarantee, the whole cost fell to me. The chance of recovering a part of it from anyone was a faint hope indeed, though I tenaciously clung to that hope for some time to come. I told Tissot to go ahead with the replacement and sat back to await developments.

Those dreary days waiting in the basin at Nevers were greatly lightened by periodic escapes into the surrounding country in the little Renault, usually on Sundays when no workmen were expected. On one of these days we made an excursion to Bourges. In the rather arbitrary grading of France's 'sights' by the Michelin green guides, Bourges rates the top category of three stars, meaning *vaut le voyage* or worth going out of your way to see. They are not wrong about Bourges, and it is the cathedral, yet another St Étienne, which has earned those three stars, and what we had come to see. Like so many French cathedrals, Bourges has a very mixed history, its construction alone stretching spasmodically over several centuries, at times with the same craftsmen also used to build the cathedrals at Soissons, Sens, Chartres and Notre-Dame in Paris. Its history is punctuated by structural failure, reconstructions, Protestant disfigurements and maladroit attempts at restoration by nineteenth-century architects. It is amazing that it could survive such an onslaught but it weathered the long tempest and exists now as one of the finest examples of French high Gothic. Purely by chance, the day of our visit was the special day of St Cecilia, the patron saint of music. On entering the cathedral we didn't know this and were overwhelmed by the crowds attending a Mass in her honour and the music from full orchestra and choir flooding through the great nave. Light was streaming down through the thirteenth-century glass high overhead, piercing the immense, dim interior with shafts of vibrating blue. It was extraordinary and moving, our senses of sight and hearing bewitched by this remarkable experience that removed us, if only briefly, from the troubles at our grubby mooring.

At long last the wait appeared to be nearing an end with the arrival, from Brest, of the new generator. Rather feeble efforts were now made to remove the old one. It was a heavy piece of equipment and, after much grunting, shoving, cursing and dropping of things into the oily bilge, Tissot and his helper appeared beaten. I suggested a different method and a simple lifting device. With this, some oil drums and a heavy piece of timber they finally extracted the dead generator, placing it on the deck as a future 'Exhibit A' in the hopeless legal offensive I would later launch. So far so good. The new generator was lowered into the engine-room and Tissot went home. One evening a day or so later, a sad-faced Tissot returned to the boat after dark to report *un petit problème*. I should have known. The coupling to connect the generator to its diesel motor was the wrong type. The right one would take several days to get and once again I sat back to wait.

Because the Loire lay between the town centre and our mooring, we had to cross a long bridge going to and from the shops. It was the main access to the town from the west, frequently congested with traffic, but one day as I was returning to the boat by car, this congestion was far worse than normal. I couldn't understand why until reaching the west end of the bridge, I came upon a bunch of irate farmers staging a

demonstration. Traffic slowed down to a crawl, then stopped entirely
for twenty minutes at a time as the farmers distributed leaflets to the
drivers of cars slowly moving past. Unwisely I signalled through the
closed window that I didn't want a leaflet. A large, red-faced man
approached the car in a purposeful way, setting off Joss, my spotted
passenger, to barking and growling. This didn't please the men around
the car much and now, clearly angry, they started banging heavily on
the car with their hands. Judging this no moment to make a stand, I
rolled down the window a bit and weakly took the leaflet thrust at my
face.

Although this was only a minor case, French demonstrations tend to
be disruptive and sometimes violent. A few months later, on our way
south on the autoroute, all traffic on this heavily travelled highway was
blocked by a small band of disaffected workers from a nearby factory.
As a result we were all shunted on to little country roads ill-suited to
cope with the sudden load. Hundreds of cars and large trailer trucks sat
for hours in a hopeless rural traffic jam that the police would not or
could not straighten out. And once, in the south of France, I saw every
piece of glass in the railway station of a major town smashed by
demonstrators. On yet another occasion, in an unthinking protest
against the British government, an attempt was made by a masked gang
to burn all two hundred boats of a British hire-boat company. The
French demonstrator is not a person to be taken lightly.

We had, by this time, been in Nevers for three weeks and, surprisingly, had managed to eke out the water supply we'd arrived with. It was now getting very low and with no other source available, stringent measures were in force to conserve the little we had. Our water needs were kept to an absolute minimum, even washing now becoming a pretty sketchy routine. It was ironic that, having waited months for a shower to be installed on *Lionel*, it had only received its finishing touches just before leaving Auxerre and now couldn't be used at all. But water wasn't our only concern. By the middle of December it had become very cold. The heating system was more or less under control provided we could get fuel and provided the portable generator continued to work. There was a little doubt about the latter when, early one morning, Melodie pulled the starting rope out by its roots, but it was repaired with difficulty by the captain and we were back in business again with hot water circulating through the radiators. And we always had the faithful little ETs to fall back on if the furnace really failed.

At last the new generator was installed and properly joined to the motor which drives it. I paid the enormous bill and foolishly believed that all generator worries were now behind me. The next day Jeremy came again from Auxerre, working late to install a new radiator in the wheelhouse and an inverter with sophisticated controls for the furnace. The latter cleverly converts 24V DC current from the batteries to 220V AC current for the oil furnace and circulating pump. This was an especial boon for early rising Melodie who could now start the furnace in the morning merely by turning a switch. We gave our helpful friend lunch and dinner, sending him on his way at midnight to drive back to Auxerre with flowers for his lady and a bottle of whisky for himself. We were much in Jeremy's debt for his support over those days at Nevers.

It was colder than normal during that December. Ice was forming rapidly in the basin and a new fear began to invade our waking hours. Already an inch thick, in a solid sheet from shore to shore, the ice was getting thicker by the hour. How ghastly it would be, we thought, to be trapped here for the winter beside those huge chalked genitalia! At all costs that was to be avoided. Soon the ice would be thick enough to skate on as we heard it had been the previous year. Ice like that would greatly discourage water travel and winter sports had no strong appeal for us just then. But the locks further along the canal were still functioning due to the flow of water through them and, although there was ice in the main canal beyond, it had recently been broken by the passage of a barge.

Our problem, therefore, centred on the basin itself and we took immediate steps to ensure our escape. Having broken as much ice as we could around the boat and leaving only the bow mooring line in place, I started the main engine, put the rudder hard over to turn the boat into the quay and, with the engine in gear, pushed the throttle forward. The effect of this was to push the stern out. When stopped by the two-inch-thick ice, we broke some more and tried again. Soon the stern was out far enough, the bow line was released and I backed the boat out so that there was room to turn it going forward. *Lionel* then became an ice-breaker with its sharp bows cleaving the ice as we joyously cruised up and down the basin smashing it into little pieces before mooring again with the bow facing our escape route.

Frozen ropes

Running a boat in winter is not everyone's idea of fun. There is certainly discomfort, even hardship, and working through a lock in sub-freezing temperatures can, at times, be really nasty. There is no denying this but the winter offers compensations and experiences that are unknown to the summer voyager. The canal in winter is at rest with little traffic to disturb its peace; the trees are bare, the fields asleep. Gone is the rich green growth of summer, but to compensate for the loss, views of country hitherto unseen open up beyond the banks and the leafless trees and bushes along the canal reveal not only their own intricate structures but also the birds that inhabit them. And the winter adds its own enrichments in the patterns of snow on branches, the sun sparkled ice, the distant white hills. The winter landscape, in its way, is as rich as that of summer and surprisingly full of life. Many of the familiar birds are still about, perhaps late starters or not migrants at all. In very cold weather during December I saw sparrow hawks, a red kite, buzzards, tufted ducks, mallards, coots, the ubiquitous carrion crow, little chaffinches, tree sparrows and linnets, wood pigeons, wrens and the occasional iridescent turquoise kingfisher. And there were lots of grey herons, flying in front of the boat, holding small meetings on the canal bank or flopping clumsily into the water after fish.

As we came out of the last lock at Nevers and entered the Canal Latéral à la Loire we encountered ice two inches thick. It covered the entire surface, cracked earlier into huge cakes by the passage of a barge. As we banged and crashed our way through it, the great sheets shivered with the impact, even thirty yards from the bow, and smaller pieces, breaking off, were sent skittering over the surface in all directions, flashing like crystal in the sun. Up in the bow, the crunch of the ice against the steel hull and the metallic tinkling noises made by the small bits of ice sliding away were appealing and unfamiliar sounds that had a startling beauty of their own. Later, we found a price had been paid for this aesthetic experience, much of the paint having been removed along the waterline.

One of the peculiarities of winter water-travel, we discovered, was the behaviour of ropes. When going through locks, ropes get wet. There is no way to avoid this, wet ropes normally being no problem in any case, apart from getting heavier, and ours, being nylon, dried quickly. In the winter, however, it is another story. When the temperature falls below freezing and wet ropes are left on deck all night, one is faced in the morning with totally unmanageable rigid coils, every kink and twist made iron by frost. If straight, a rope in this state would undoubtedly stand upright but, straight or coiled, it is useless. It can't be tied in knots, thrown or fastened in any useful fashion. When this first happened, there was nothing to be done but replace them with old ones from *Lionel's* reserves and afterwards, the ropes not being used for mooring were always brought into the wheelhouse overnight where they lay in ungainly, damp heaps waiting to be tripped over.

The Crew

The Captain

Because of our late departure from Auxerre and the delay at Nevers we were experiencing more severe winter conditions than expected. Not only did the ropes freeze but the boat was often covered in snow, making treacherous the various places where Melodie perched before jumping off at locks. These had to be carefully scraped to remove all ice and snow before they were safe to use. Even getting water became a difficult matter with many of the canalside taps turned off for the winter. The boat itself was warm enough, although we didn't use the furnace, relying mainly on Melodie's faithful little ETs and, while running during the day, heat from the main engine below kept the wheelhouse warm. Supplements of good food and wine did the rest.

The exigencies of winter canal travel did, however, expose some weaknesses in our clothing, or more precisely, Melodie's, which had to be corrected along the way. We both had adequate parkas to keep us warm and dry, allowing also the free movement necessary for jumping and throwing ropes. But Melodie's extremities seemed, in those days, to be always either wet or cold and generally both. Starting with our feet, we both had those rubber-boots designed for limited use aboard elegant yachts. Being waterproof and non-slip they are good for that purpose but soon spring leaks when exposed day after day to the hard gritty surfaces of towpaths and locks. They are also cold. Although Melodie bought some 'long johns' in Nevers to keep her legs warm she didn't solve the foot problem until later, in Lyon, where she found some stout rubber-boots complete with warm liners. Constantly wet feet are cold feet and it was the same with Melodie's hands. Wet ropes and ladders soon soaked her mitts, wool, leather or whatever and by the middle of the day every mitt or glove she owned was soaking wet, lying all over the wheelhouse in a hopeful but vain attempt to dry them. This problem was also solved in Lyon at the wonderful barge emporium with the purchase of heavy black industrial rubber gloves which Melodie could wear over warm woollen liners. It seemed to take an inordinate amount of time for Melodie to resolve her clothing problems but, once done, she faced the perils of winter like a different woman.

We came, at last, to the end of the Canal Latéral à la Loire at Digoin after crossing a long aqueduct just before the town. A place of no interest and little charm, Digoin had at least one surprising feature for such a small and undistinguished place. After doing some quiet, almost clandestine, research in the red *Guide Michelin* Melodie reported, with heavy hints, that Digoin, in spite of the way it looked, contained, somewhere within its fabric, a priceless jewel, a two-star restaurant. And it was true enough; just down the street from our mooring, in this unlikely town, was a most elegant temple of *la nouvelle cuisine*. By this time, having endured much, we were ripe for such a treat. For me, Digoin will always be the memory of the delicious and extravagant dinner we enjoyed there on the night of our arrival. I can recall the mysterious hot little *délices* blended of herbs, goat's cheese and nuts that accompanied the Kir to start the meal, the pleasure to eye and palate of each course placed before us with such panache by the young waiter, the little *salade tiède* of *endive* and lamb's kidney, the marinated trout and egg plant, the thinly sliced, barely cooked *filet de boeuf* under a delicate mildly spicy sauce that defied analysis. In a meal of nine courses it is difficult to remember all of them but the last dish of all stands out above the others, pears and a kind of pound cake served hot in a ramekin dish with a delicate, seedless raspberry sauce. After that we were ready for anything that winter might throw our way.

The Canal du Centre which goes north-east from Digoin was built in the late eighteenth century but much changed a hundred years later. It has sixty-one locks and a character all its own. The canal winds through open, rolling farmland and forest with sweeping views of the country through the canalside trees, leafless but for great globes of mistletoe scattered among their branches. It is a busy canal in normal times, the favoured route of barges between the Seine and the Saône or the Rhône further south. This traffic has had a pronounced influence on the canal. The lock-keepers who must work long hours are younger than usual and go about their business with an efficiency and dispatch rarely found in this trade. The *marinier* is also helped on his way by the locks themselves, most of which have been electrified, and many in the southern part are completely automatic with devices that 'see' an approaching boat and get the lock prepared.

At these latter locks there are no lock-keepers, only controls to operate the lock. All this is wonderfully efficient and speeds progress but I regret the passing of the lock-keeper with his family, his dogs and his garden. In the new automatic locks there is usually a lifeless house, no friendly soul to chat to, no news of canal events, no way of discovering what barges one is likely to meet, no vegetables or wine for sale, no dogs sniffing and barking at the lockside. The canals will be far less interesting places when the lock-keepers have all gone as they assuredly will. But the few who remain on the Canal du Centre are a pretty good bunch, so different from those on the Yonne. One of them, seeing our Canadian flag, was full of his earlier trip to Canada and the snowshoes he still treasured from that visit. Before we left his lock he made us sample a potent, home-brewed *eau de vie* made from plums: strong stuff so early in the day but not unwelcome in the freezing cold.

Passing through the locks of this canal was easy and made even more so by the fact that most were ready when we arrived, due either to the 'seeing' devices or because a barge had just passed going in the opposite direction. It was very smooth sailing, even twenty locks in one day putting no strain on the crew, and only once a minor problem, the result of carelessness. While chatting to a lock-keeper and a visiting canal inspector, I allowed the boat to drift so far over to one side of the lock that the counter overhung the lockside and became hung up as the water lowered, tilting the boat alarmingly. I rushed into the wheelhouse, pushing the throttle forward and forcing the boat off the wall. It sloshed back heavily into the water and danced around for a while, causing some alarm among the surprised bystanders. More serious trouble was avoided because the engine was still running. Perhaps due to fears about fire some waterway authorities in Canada and England insist that engines be stopped in locks. I am glad there is no such rule in France.

It was on the Canal du Centre that the generator, so recently the cause of much annoyance and pain, struck once again, refusing to start one morning for its own odd reasons. In Montceau-les-Mines I found an electrician to render first aid. He did not seem a very promising candidate when I first saw him in his minuscule and utterly chaotic car repair garage. Italian by birth, dreadfully overworked, unshaven and speaking an almost unintelligible French, he nevertheless knew his business, saw immediately what was wrong and promptly fixed it. You can't ask for more than that. The generator, however, continued to play its little tricks. This time there was no problem starting the damn thing but it refused one day to stop in response to the normal wheelhouse controls. For the next several weeks the only means I had of bringing the wretched machine to a halt was to go down into the engine-room and throttle its plastic fuel line with a pair of pliers. When, I thought, would my generator troubles ever end?

Like most canals, the Canal du Centre has its share of sharp corners. One may dreamily approach these in the belief that nothing is coming the other way, but it often is and a little caution pays handsomely in preventing frayed tempers and perhaps bent metal. Being alert to the possibility, however, never seems to lessen the surprise of these corner confrontations. One is suddenly faced with a massive steel bow pushing purposefully through the water to what seems certain collision with one's own boat. And it probably is. At this moment it is important to know that barges, especially loaded ones, are heavy, slow to stop, difficult to turn sharply and restricted, more or less, to the centre of the canal. Any evasive manoeuvres must consequently be taken largely by the smaller boat. It is obvious that two loaded barges, meeting on a sharp corner in a narrow, shallow canal, aggravate the problem mightily. We met such a situation during one of our last days on the Canal du Centre.

In an effort to squeeze past each other, one of them went aground. At this moment the two *mariniers* appeared to put their troubles to one side, settling down instead to a good chat over several glasses of wine. There was no way we could pass them and, moored with grapnels to bushes on the bank, we waited impatiently the thirty minutes or so it took for their impromptu 'happy hour' to come to an end. Eventually one barge freed itself and left, leaving the other angled across the canal. We had waited long enough, so judging there was room, I sneaked *Lionel* past with inches to spare. The young *marinier*, thinking wrongly that I had scraped a flake of paint off his barge, stormed out of his wheelhouse, down the full length of the deck waving his arms and shouting abuse at us as we passed. I'm sure a wine-enhanced resentment of pleasure boats lay behind his unjustified behaviour and I could do little but continue carefully past the barge mouthing quiet oaths to myself in the shelter of the wheelhouse.

In our experience, this kind of thing is rare. The working men and women of the waterways are normally tolerant of those who are there for pleasure, providing the commercial barges can get on with their job without undue interference from the *plaisancier*. The two can exist peacefully together in a live-and-let-live relationship, but the *marinier* is about serious business affecting his already precarious livelihood and should not be expected to tolerate delays caused by pleasure boaters with time on their hands.

Mighty rivers

The last lock on the Canal du Centre is a fitting climax to that waterway, having a drop of nearly thirty-five feet down to the level of the Saône where one arrives through a curtain of dripping water from the raised guillotine gate at its lower end. That the Saône is one of the great rivers of France is all too evident to anyone who has just arrived in it after spending days in the linear confinement of a canal. This calm, spacious river, rising in the Vosges mountains to the east, joins the Rhône at Lyon, thus forming an important link in the great waterway that will one day carry large commercial craft on an inland route between the Mediterranean and northern Europe. Only the old canal between the Saône and the Rhine now stands in the way, but it will one day be reconstructed to the required 'European standard', thus completing the route.

In normal times the Saône is a quiet river with a moderate current resulting from its shallow gradient but, like all rivers, it is prone to flooding and water levels can sometimes rise dramatically in a few hours. It also has a few navigational hazards, in the form of submerged stone training walls, designed to direct the current and keep the channel free of silt. These are normally no problem if one remains within the channel markers but they have claimed the occasional victim rash enough to take his chances outside them. Our friend, Johnny, in his barge the *Amity Belle* suffered this fate when forced out of the channel by what he felt was certain collision with a barge, and ran on to a training wall, putting a hole in the steel hull and barely making it to port in St Jean de Losne. Clearly, even this benign river should not be treated casually.

Our start on the Saône was inauspicious. We had been warned about the stepped quay of Chalon and recommended to use a mooring at or near a marina behind an island on the other side of the river. Because *Lionel*, big and heavy, can cause damage to small boats in marinas, we decided to moor against the bank nearby. It was not a promising spot: a bare, wet, slippery, clay bank sloped down to a narrow concrete wall at the shore where rocks were plainly visible in the shallow water. It was either here or somewhere a good deal worse so I made our approach, Melodie somehow scrambling ashore with a rope. It was raining and a brisk wind was blowing offshore, thwarting Melodie's strenuous efforts to close the gap between boat and shore, a hateful predicament for her. There was little I could do to help as she tried to remain upright on the treacherous bank with the rope, feebly anchored to a ridiculous birch sapling, slowly stretching as the boat moved away from her. Somehow, with enormous effort and almost in tears, she managed to pull the boat close enough for me to get ashore with another rope, our combined pull at last achieving results and we moored as best we could. All through the night *Lionel* bumped and scraped gently against the rocks although by then there was little we could do about it.

At Tournus, the next day, we were to experience the volatility of the Saône for the first time, mooring below the town where the water on our arrival was only five inches below the top of the quay. But it had been raining further up the river and the water started to rise, lapping over the quay an hour or two later. By the time we had been into town to shop and visit the magnificent Romanesque abbey church of St Philibert, it was right over the quay and still rising. We then took preventive measures similar to those taken in Auxerre some time before, lashing two steel poles vertically to the boat with their ends on the river bottom. The precautions worked well, even standing up to the buffeting from passing barges and we were soon joined by a small French yacht en route to the Azores crewed by a young doctor and his girl friend, a nurse. They moored beside us and later came to dinner.

Social evenings entirely in French are not easy for us but this one was easier than many because of the way our guests spoke their language, both clearly and, I'm sure, at slower than normal speed. Although I can claim a larger stock of French words and a better grasp of grammar, it is really Melodie who has the greater fluency, guileless though it may be, casting aside all the rules and the limitations of a minuscule vocabulary. She just wants to talk to people and nothing, not even a strange language, is going to get in her way. I have often marvelled at her chatting away to people for twenty minutes at a stretch about God knows what. Her eagerness to talk overrides everything, even her insistent distortion of some common expressions. Although *Lionel* is a barge, it is also a pleasure boat, *un bateau de plaisance* in French. But Melodie has never got this quite right and insists on calling it *un bateau de plaisir*. This has an entirely different meaning which prompts very odd looks from French listeners. I suppose I will never wean her away from this description of our boat as a floating brothel!

Throughout the night at Tournus the water continued to rise, one of us having to get up every two hours to make sure all was well. In the morning the quay was about two feet under water and Joss was unable to go ashore, having to resign herself unwillingly to using the deck. Our eventual departure from this watery mooring had more the hallmarks of slapstick comedy than the unobtrusive, quiet efficiency of the captain's fantasies. It was an awful 'we must never do that again' kind of thing. We released the mooring lines from their now subaqueous bollards, stupidly leaving the steel poles in place, fearing the boat might still float on to the submerged quay. One pole was brought aboard but as the second one was being shipped, the current took the untethered boat, swinging it around 90 degrees to the quay and as we hurried to get the second pole aboard, we came close to smashing several wheelhouse windows. It could have been worse but was certainly bad enough for a crew who should have known better. I suppose it is a truth about boats that in spite of their crew's experience and constant watchfulness they will always find an unexpected way to make a fool of one.

The remainder of the journey down the Saône was without major incident. The weather was good, a weak winter sun low in the sky trying very hard to cheer things up as we cruised south, covering fifty to seventy miles a day. After an overnight stop at Mâcon, where an unfriendly fate always puts our mooring too close to the pungent quayside *pissoir*, we continued downriver to Lyon which soon came into sight. Past the last lock near the city outskirts we ran parallel to a small and seemingly harmless day tour boat on its way into the lock at full speed. I paid it little attention and took no precautions. This was a mistake. To my surprise the boat's wash was grossly out of proportion to its size and I was quite unprepared for the ranks of short, five-foot waves that came charging at us broadside. As we rolled and plunged through them it was like being briefly at sea with water breaking over the bow and smashing down on the deck. *Lionel* took it well and I'm sure could handle far worse than this but I have no wish to put it to the test.

As we slipped under bridge after bridge into the centre of Lyon it was a little like the Seine in Paris with a wall of nineteenth-century buildings lining both sides of the river above high stone quays. But Lyon was to prove an entirely different kind of city, smaller in scale and with its own special flavour, touched slightly perhaps by the climate and attitudes of the south. It is magnificently sited on the eastern edge of the Massif Central at the confluence of two great rivers, the Saône and the Rhône, and has been a place of importance since Roman times. Although now the second city of France, Lyon had industrial importance in the seventeenth century when it became a major centre of silk-weaving, until then almost an Italian monopoly. This industrial growth was greatly accelerated two hundred years later with Jacquard's invention here of a loom that required only one weaver to do the work that formerly needed six. Lyon is also famous as the hometown of Ampère, the physicist, whose work in the field of electrodynamics has made his name a household word, and Lumière, the father of cinematography, did much of his work here. Lyon claims, as well, to be the birthplace of *boules*, and it was near Lyon that the first use was made of something that later came to be known as a parachute. One of the Montgolfier brothers, of hot-air balloon fame, ascended to a height of over a hundred feet and released a presumably terrified sheep in a wicker basket supported by nothing more than an oversized parasol. The experiment was thought by all to have been a success. The passenger may have viewed the matter differently but survived nevertheless.

Lyon is a vigorous, modern metropolis with all the resources and amenities one could wish. It was refreshing for us to be once again in such a vibrant urban milieu. Although our stay on this occasion was short we explored much of the town on foot; the busy, sophisticated centre, the old quarter across the river and Fourvière at the top of the hill on the west side of the Saône. From there the great city lies below with the faint outline of hills far to the east, distant forerunners of the Alps. At Fourvière too was the incredible nineteenth-century cathedral built by the Lyonnais to give thanks to the Almighty for their escape from occupation by the Germans in the war of 1870. No expense was spared in the building of this extraordinary artefact but it has an air of pretension about it, seeming to be more a monument to the affluent Lyonnais bourgeoisie of the time than to anything more exalted.

Lyon has a reputation for good food. I don't know whether this is really deserved or not but the city is certainly well supplied with expensive restaurants boasting two or three of the coveted Michelin stars: Paul Bocuse is just upstream on the Saône and 'La Pyramide' not far away in the other direction at Vienne. Our limited experience, however, would do nothing to reinforce this reputation although the sampling was so small as to have no significance. Being in Lyon over Christmas we chose to have a *réveillon* dinner on Christmas Eve in a packed, unpretentious little restaurant not far from our mooring at Perrache. Dish followed dish in a stomach-jamming sequence that, as always, put me in awe of the French capacity to tuck away food. I recall eating overcooked wild boar and a separate vegetable that had the appearance and texture of thistle and was as palatable. Both are traditional *réveillon* dishes as, perhaps, were some of the others which I can no longer remember. But whatever they were, the meal was not a gastronomic experience to cherish and we left feeling that Lyon deserved to be given another chance at some later time.

Before leaving Lyon for the journey down the Rhône we stopped to refuel at the barges downstream of the Perrache railway bridge, a combined service station and ships' chandler's, catering to the needs of *mariniers*. There are two barges tied side by side, one for fuel and the other containing a store in its cavernous belly. What a bonanza! Here one can find everything a barge might need from light bulbs, fuses, glue, paint, searchlights, wood bumpers, brooms, charts, clothing, hardware, and a hundred other things all the way to chains, cable and heavy rope. It is a wonderful place and a vicious, temptingly baited trap I can never resist. We loaded up with red diesel fuel for the generator and furnace and the more expensive white which French regulations insist be used for the main engine, the distinction being rigidly enforced by *les douanes* who happily slap punitive fines on cheats.

Soon the city was behind us and we entered the Rhône, a mighty river by any standard. Born in the alpine snows, it flows through Lac Léman in Switzerland, leaves it at Geneva and continues into France, becoming navigable just east of Lyon and remaining so for the next two hundred miles of its journey south to the Mediterranean. Ever since used by man the Rhône has had a bad reputation: accidents and disasters have darkened its history stretching back to the days when fifty or more horses were needed to haul boats upstream against the current. Over recent years much of the hazard of the river, and some of its interest as well, has been removed by the great canalization scheme undertaken by the French government to control the river, provide irrigation and generate electricity. Finally completed in 1980, the series of long, boring canal cuts, weirs, power stations, giant locks and the general deepening of the navigable channel have done much to control the treacherous current. But it remains a river with tricks up its sleeve for the unwary navigator. The current is still strong, mooring places scarce and the Mistral continues to blow hard from the north, sometimes for days on end, creating waves that can trouble a small boat.

The first thing one notices about the Rhône is space. The river and the landscape on either side of it are on a large scale. The river is so wide that, for a change, one can relax a bit at the wheel and spend time gazing at the passing countryside, a luxury rarely enjoyed on narrow canals or even parts of the Saône. And there are no high banks, barriers of bushes or trees to impede views sweeping away on both sides to distant blue hills, a most refreshing change after the almost claustrophobic intimacy of some canals. As one would expect, everything about the Rhône is in scale with the river itself. The basic facts are impressive enough: of the twelve locks the shallowest has a lift of close to twenty feet, most are far in excess of this and the one at Bollène just short of eighty-six feet. Each is 640 feet long, forty feet wide and equipped with floating bollards that rise and fall with the water. It is an experience to pass through one of these locks, the water sinking surprisingly fast, with little turbulence, to drop the boat down to the bottom of the enormous, dripping, concrete cavern. Then the giant guillotine gates, filling the entire end of the lock, slowly rise to reveal once again a glimpse of the outside world and the river ahead. It all happens with efficient, mechanical anonymity and with little sound but for the squeaking and groaning of the bollards sliding in their tracks. The lock-keeper remains high overhead and remote in his cabin, cut off from contact with the boats far below except by loudspeaker and VHF radio.

The traffic in and out of these locks is controlled by lights. As we travelled south with the low winter sun reflecting off the water it was difficult to see these lights, even with binoculars. We tried to improve things with dark glasses, even Polaroid ones, but the improvement was only slight and we often had to get very close to the lock before seeing if the lights were green, red or both, the last indicating that the lock was being prepared. Since a wait outside the locks was often necessary, the mooring facilities there became very familiar territory to us, exposing shortcomings that often made life difficult for *Lionel*'s crew. Good moorings outside river locks, particularly at the exposed upstream end, are always important but especially on the Rhône, whose large surface is often swept by strong winds. What has been provided is a row of what the French call *Ducs d'Albe*. It is a strange name for a strange device, each one being a tripod of large steel pipes driven into the river bed, tied together and fitted with little bollards. The Dukes of Alba are placed so far apart that any boat shorter than a commercial barge is forced to moor to one tripod only. And to make matters worse, the Dukes of Alba are oddly installed with the single pipe on the mooring side. Once moored to such a thing, the boat swings constantly at the whim of wind and current, requiring continuous use of rudder and screw to keep it even moderately straight. This is bad enough but to add a little extra zest to the experience, the 'authorities' have dispersed among the Dukes a sprinkling of trick bollards. Some are cleverly concealed, proving difficult to find in the few seconds that may be available for this task, some have special surprise rope-releasing properties and a few are even mounted upside down to test the quick thinking of sleepier crew members.

One can cover great daily distances on the Rhône, especially when going south with the current. Without pushing it we covered sixty to seventy-five miles a day and it would not be difficult to exceed this substantially. Even the old passenger boats only took one day to do the whole distance from Lyon to Arles in Provence. The commonest adversary on the Rhône, and the one that can sometimes slow progress, is wind, either from the south or the north, though generally the latter, the Mistral, that cold wind that blows down the Rhône valley from the Alps. It is then that waiting for a lock at the upstream end can become trying. There is no shelter from the lock structures as at the downstream side and one is exposed to the full blast of whatever wind is blowing. Mooring becomes very difficult, making it prudent, at times, to remain secure in some safe place until the wind has abated.

But, as we cruised south, the wind was not a bother apart from a southerly breeze against the current scuffing up a little chop. The weather was good, the December sun doing its feeble best to welcome us to the south, its atmosphere slowly but surely asserting itself in a gradual but noticeable change in the temperature, the hours of sun each day, the terrain and the architecture. The tiled roofs of Provence, the increasing warmth, the dry earth and sparse growth were all signals, as were the birds. Gone was the intimate habitat of the northern waterways to be replaced the further South we went by wide open countryside already showing hints of the Mediterranean still some distance away.

Water birds of all kinds were now around us in profusion; common, black-headed and herring gulls, mute swans, mallards, shovellers, teal, cormorants and once a plenary session of forty grey herons standing solemnly on the sloping bank of a canal cut. But the herons were becoming rarer and the cormorants were now our favourites, perching on the channel markers, often with wings outstretched, looking like heraldic symbols. The cormorant is a diver by trade but by some twist of fate appears not to have been given an adequate way of keeping its feathers waterproof like other aquatic birds. When it dives for the fish it must eat, it returns to the air wetter than it would like and must hang its wings out to dry. These wings are a problem in another way, a problem it shares with the North American Loon, both birds being compromise designs, built for both air and under-water travel. And both are large, heavy birds with long thin wings resulting in what an aeronautical engineer would call 'high wing loading'. Because of this the cormorant has trouble getting into the air and must fly fast to remain airborne. Even from the top of channel markers on the Rhône, the cormorants seemed to need the ten-foot drop to water level before their flight was sustained and a water take-off appears to be a struggle, especially in the absence of wind.

In almost no time we had arrived in Avignon where we remained for the night only having visited the town on other occasions. We left early

87

the following day in blurry sunshine on the final leg of our Rhône journey, coming shortly to the last lock before turning off the river. The lock-keeper, a jovial and optimistic soul, shouted as we left his lock: 'The sun always shines in Provence.' With his confident weather forecast still ringing in our ears we sailed happily down the river to encounter only ten minutes later a wall of impenetrable fog. Thinking at first it was only local pollution from a nearby cellulose factory we carried on blindly hoping to break through the cotton-wool. But we didn't. It was clearly madness to be navigating on that river in such conditions and regardless of the hazards that anchoring or mooring might present, they seemed a great deal less than bumbling along in zero visibility. So I decided to moor out of the channel, against the bank, wherever it might be. I turned *Lionel* to bring its bow into the current and approached the bank very, very slowly with Melodie poised in the bow to release the anchor at a signal from me. I didn't know what was going to happen but felt sure that, at the very least, we would hit bottom and prayed that it would be made of something softer than unyielding rock. To our surprise, we didn't hit anything at all. There was lots of water under the keel right to the shore where, at the last minute, a convenient tree offered itself for mooring. We remained tied to that tree, the only secure thing in a very uncertain world, for several hours, until there was enough visibility to continue cautiously down the river.

We were now approaching one of the trickier parts of the journey. It was in a narrow part of the Rhône with a very strong current running that we had to turn off the main river on to the Petit Rhône. With Melodie once again in the bow peering ahead through the fog with binoculars we picked our way slowly downstream, carefully counting the channel markers appearing through the murk one at a time and hoping that our sketchy Vagnon chart of the river was reasonably accurate. Everything was subtle shades of grey: the water, the sky, the trees along the shore. I felt that if I didn't concentrate hard on the fine distinctions between them they would all blend into one fuzzy mess and we'd be completely lost again. Because of what I assumed were trees, the shore was a slightly darker grey than the rest and it was this fact that saved the day. As we passed what the entire crew agreed must be the last channel marker before the turn, I detected a faint lighter grey gap in the darker grey of the shoreline. This had to be the Petit Rhône and I turned the boat into it. Praise be to St Nicholas, the patron saint of mariners, the Petit Rhône indeed it was.

But the fog was again getting worse. Although we kept going for a while, the channel markers barely visible on either side, it was crazy to go on. So, once again, I turned the boat and brought it into the shore. We didn't go aground but the bank was very steep and covered in brambles. Melodie got one rope around an overhanging tree and I scrambled ashore to fix another. It was an awful place, the bank was so steep and slippery that I could only stop myself sliding into the water by grabbing the brambles, returning to the boat, at last, scratched and exhausted.

The view down the Petit Rhône the next morning was clear and bright with the striped channel markers standing out sharply, recalling the mooring posts on Venice's Grand Canal. We were now near the end of our journey with just one more lock at St Gilles and then the long, boring, overgrown canal leading up to Beaucaire where we arrived in the afternoon of New Year's Eve, 1983. There was a high wind blowing as we entered the port. Because of this and uncertainty about our eventual mooring we moored in the first available place, going slightly aground in so doing. I didn't give it much thought at the time, for this is common enough on canals but by the following morning the water in the canal had dropped by a surprising twelve inches, leaving *Lionel* truly aground, with a 20 degree list to port. The explanation given for this strange phenomenon was the use of canal water for irrigation of nearby vineyards but whatever the reason, we were in a ridiculous predicament and remained in it for the next two days. To make matters

worse, our mooring happened to be beside the outlet of a town drain and the listing boat had put the water intake of the WC above water level, adding an unwanted element of complexity to daily routines. The police came to enquire after our welfare but there was little they or anyone could do to change the *status quo*. Only rising water would do that and, at last, it did. It was not a happy introduction to Beaucaire and Melodie, who has no love for rivers, was forced to admit that even her safe old canals can sometimes kick one in the teeth.

Beaucaire

Having decided to spend the winter in the south of France, Beaucaire had appealed to us as a first stopping place on the basis of hearsay more than anything else. There was also the promise of seeing old friends and the enticement of shore power, always a potent drawing card. The shore power turned out to be nothing more than a dream but the friends were there and that was more important.

Midway between Avignon and Arles, the twin towns of Tarascon and Beaucaire sit astride the Rhône, both, at one time, significant strongholds with massive stone fortresses guarding the river. Tarascon, the smaller of the two, was put on the literary map by the French writer Daudet, whose book, *Tartarin de Tarascon*, I remember struggling through at school many years ago. Beaucaire has no matching literary ties but once was a major port and from the thirteenth to the nineteenth centuries had an enormous annual fair attracting several hundred thousand visitors. Because of recent river changes, direct water access to Beaucaire no longer exists and its status has diminished to that of a small provincial town supporting some industry but acting mainly as the centre of the surrounding wine-growing area.

Beaucaire was a far cry from the peaceful haven we had known at Auxerre. Most unfortunately all east- and west-bound cars and trucks were funnelled through the port area on their way to and from the only bridge over the Rhône, creating a raucous, restless, roaring vortex of traffic around the short stretch of canal where boats were moored. The quietest mooring was on a part of the canal that once connected to the river but it was already filled with boats, a kind of select residential precinct unavailable to lesser folk.

Then there was the Mistral, that nasty, nerve-jangling wind that the natives claim blows for three, six or nine days at a time and with which I established an enduring enmity. In Beaucaire, I suppose the definitive Mistral experience was to cross the Rhône to Tarascon on foot with the wind at full force, holding the wind-sock on the bridge

91

rigidly horizontal as if made of steel. The braver types, attempting the crossing, leaned steeply into the blast, one hand grasping the railing, their loose hair and clothing pulled out straight by the wind as they battled their way across. In the port of Beaucaire, due apparently to the quirky effect of local hills, the Mistral became a wind from the west, blowing right down the canal, a fact with which we were both to become intimately familiar during the coming days as we worked outside on *Lionel*. Although Melodie was not so affected by the Mistral, my own experience amply confirmed its reputation as an irritant well able to transform sensitive souls into nail-biting nervous wrecks. But we endured the wind and, in the following weeks, our first impressions lost much of their negative thrust as we came to know Beaucaire better, the town revealing more than we'd expected to discover and enjoy. But that came later. The first few days were full of refloating the boat, making ourselves at home in a new mooring, recovering the car from Lyon, dealing with a mountain of accumulated mail, seeing old friends and getting to know new ones.

In my mind, the two words Beaucaire and generator are almost synonymous, mention of one always conjuring up unpleasant visions of the other, for it was in this town that the second bout of serious generator trouble took place. Since the promise of shore power in the port had turned out to be illusory, the generator once again leapt into the limelight to assume its leading role in the hierarchy of power aboard *Lionel*. The opening skirmishes with the generator were child's play compared to what would follow in this machine's pockmarked career of unreliability but they would do for starters. In an idle moment on the way south I had gone to the engine-room to clean the generator's air-filter, but, after removing the covering panels, was surprised to find the filter missing. I later found it lying in a corner of the engine-room in unusable, broken pieces where, no doubt, it had been angrily flung by some inept mechanic whose identity I could only guess at. I had subsequently ordered a new filter which had been delivered to Beaucaire and I set about installing it.

As so often happens, what appears easy in prospect transforms rapidly, under my hands, into fiendish, time-consuming complexity. The framework of the sound-insulating-box around the generator was in the way of easy installation so I set about modifications. It was a poor decision. Several miserable hours followed as I lay curled up uncomfortably in an almost inaccessible part of the engine-room cutting steel away with a grinder that spat metal fragments and sparks at my face. But the air-filter was at last installed. I retired dirty, fatigued and bruised to the wheelhouse where I started the generator. Almost immediately the engine-room filled with dense blue exhaust fumes. Too exhausted then to cope with yet another problem, I returned the next morning, unravelled the asbestos wrapping around the exhaust pipe and, not surprisingly, found it broken. Was this the same mad mechanic at work again? The exhaust pipe was repaired by a local welder, broke again and was finally repaired again, this time with a proper flexible section acquired at great expense from one of the gold-plated Paris ships' chandler's. Was this generator ever going to function properly? Might it fail me entirely? What was going to happen next?

The generator had always been a very lethargic machine, needing to be wound over and over by the battery before sauntering reluctantly into a kind of life. Following the suggestion of a friend I checked the fuel line for leaks, finding no fewer than three and replacing it with one-piece copper pipe. After that things went well for a while until one day the miserable thing refused to start again. This time I found all the wires to the ignition key had come out. Why? By trial and error the wires were re-connected and I waited with resignation for the next calamity to strike. When it came, it was far more serious. One day the starter motor sank into a terminal coma from which it could not be roused. I removed the moribund *démarreur* from its awkward mounting on the generator and carried the corpse to a small garage in Tarascon where someone said it could be fixed. And there began another story.

We were now involved in a crisis that had all the marks of an earlier one: no generator, no shore power, fast dwindling batteries. Something had to be done, so I bought a small portable Honda generator as a stand-in until big brother came off the sick list. This was my first experience of these little machines which I was overjoyed to discover supplanted, in many ways, the dead monster in the engine-room, providing power to charge the batteries (if run long enough), start the furnace and operate power tools (within reason). We later acquired another slightly larger Honda, relying in future far more on these two little beasts than the large fickle number in the bowels of the boat.

In spite of the cold wind, Melodie and I worked hard on *Lionel* during our weeks at Beaucaire, she at painting the boat and I at my usual carpentry. Melodie devoted most of her time, when rain and wind permitted, to painting the boat from stem to gudgeon and waterline to top of mast. It was a big job for one person with its share of unpleasant work, particularly the hull, most of which had to be done from the boat's little plastic dinghy, a flighty, unstable platform at the best of times. Above the hull there was more pleasure in the painting, every day the boat looking better as the old colours disappeared beneath the new.

The hull was painted solid black, covering the earlier weak horizontal bands of white and navy-blue and the previously white superstructure was changed to dark-green. When the painting was finished, *Lionel* had taken on a different character, stronger and more in the tradition of its past working life, some of which we discovered for the first time at Beaucaire through two knowledgeable Dutch friends who examined *Lionel* in some detail. The boat, they were sure, had been built in the 1920s and first used to make scheduled deliveries of goods on the canals of Holland. When road transport took over this function, the boat had, apparently, been converted into a tanker or bunker boat delivering diesel fuel to barges on Dutch canals and rivers. At that time the bow was modified to deal with the waves encountered on the latter and a more powerful engine installed to counter their strong currents. It is an interesting footnote to this assumed history that such tankers were, it seems, usually painted blue. Sure enough, after scraping through several layers of paint on the deck, we came, as predicted, to a brilliant blue.

Beaucaire, like many towns in the south of the country, has gathered over time a great many people from the old French colonies of Morocco and Algeria. While some seem to have become part of French life, there are others, the more visible ones, who still look as if they had only come recently from their North African homeland. During our few weeks in Beaucaire we came to know slightly a woman of this latter group, an old Moroccan whom Melodie had first helped carry an impossible load of firewood back to her room in the town. She was a woman in her late sixties with a tattooed face and still wearing traditional clothes. She had only left her rural Moroccan village a few years before with her son, now unemployed, who lived with his wife and seven children near Beaucaire. We helped her in many ways as far as we could for she was very poor and, a few days later, I gave her, as well, a lot of wood left over from carpentry on the boat. To express her gratitude, Madame Lazibi Habiba asked us to have lunch in her second floor room in one of the back streets of the town.

We duly arrived at the house and climbed up the narrow stone stairs. Her small room had a high-beamed ceiling, one door, and one window facing the street. There was an old bed at the back of the room, a table and three chairs, some rudimentary cupboards, an old refrigerator, an ancient gas stove and a sink with no water. The only heat came from a broken cast-iron stove against one wall with flaming pieces of wood projecting dangerously from it. Madame Habiba's French was strange to our ears but we chatted away while she mixed the couscous with her henna-dyed hands, piling our plates high with it, some vegetables and a few pieces of meat, followed later by salad, fruit and the lovely mint tea of her home country. It was a simple meal but we were touched by the trouble she had taken and honoured to share it with her.

The day before we left Beaucaire, Madame Habiba arrived at the boat in her usual bedroom slippers, bringing as a gift the Moroccan rug that had been hanging on the wall of her room, its one and only embellishment. We were overwhelmed that one who had so little could offer so much in a gesture of gratitude. We didn't want to deprive her of such a precious possession but knew she would be offended by refusal. So we accepted it with our thanks and it remains on the boat to this day, a symbol of her generous spirit. Madame Habiba will long remain in our memories for her naturalness, honesty and simple dignity.

The winter was, at last, winding down. Boats were beginning to leave the port, one of the first being *Amity Belle*, followed not long after by the Dutch contingent in their immaculate barges. And then it was our turn to leave as well. Most of our friends had already gone, leaving almost no one behind to toot a horn as we slipped down the canal. But as we passed under the *passerelle* our two American friends Dee and Bill were standing there waving and throwing flowers on to *Lionel*'s deck. It was a lovely farewell, and a great improvement over the customary noisy tooting of horns.

Canal du Midi

There was little sadness aboard *Lionel* as we headed down the long canal away from Beaucaire. It had been a useful brief stopping place but much more interesting places lay on our journey further west, the first leg of which would be along the northern edge of the Camargue, the large salt-impregnated marshland between Arles and the Mediterranean. Although now partially tamed to support crops such as rice, most of the Camargue is still what it has always been, a wild place of wind-blown grasses, birds, horses and bulls. Since our route, the Canal Rhône à Sète, skirted the northern edge of the Camargue proper we had only occasional glimpses of its bird and animal life. The famous horses were to be seen grazing here and there although I wondered if the somnolent, slightly grubby creatures we saw could really be the same animals as the spirited, pure white horses of the travel posters. The bulls were very much scarcer and might have been missed entirely if we hadn't met, by chance, a herd of forty or so beside the canal in the charge of a man on horseback. These small black bulls, being raised for the bull ring, were a sporty-looking lot led by one of their number with silver balls on the tips of his horns. The horns of the rest were rapier sharp and a dangerous challenge for the men who, in some French bullfights, must risk a goring to pluck rosettes placed between the horns. In such bullfights, the bulls are not killed but instead, in what seems an appropriate reversal of the normal roles, become the stars of the show. The Camargue, however, is pre-eminently a place of birds, the resident population being large, varied and expanding dramatically during times of migration. Along the canal there were all kinds of water birds; red-headed pochard ducks, little egrets with their odd yellow feet, stone curlews, little ringed plovers and the incredible pink greater flamingos, one of the more bizarre creatures of the air. Large flocks of them stood in the shallow salt water pools beside the canal in tight companionable groups. Off to the side, like little satellites, were formations of insecure-looking grey-white adolescents as yet unsure of where they belonged. And overhead pale pink flocks of these amazing birds flew by with knobbly legs trailing behind and golf club heads a long way out in front.

The principal town on the Canal Rhône à Sète is Aigues Mortes where we stopped for the night. Its name means 'dead waters' and the old place seems to have an appropriately melancholy air about it. Built originally in the thirteenth century by the saintly French king, Louis (canonised after his death), as a base from which to launch a crusade in Palestine, it is no longer as close to the sea as it once must have been, sitting isolated now, a stone-walled trapezoid in the wide featureless Camargue flatlands. As a fortified town, Aigues Mortes is a far cry from romantic Carcassonne further to the west in site, size and design. It is an austere place, the town tightly contained within defensive walls, its narrow, dark streets ruled by a rigid military discipline. Although it seems to be an obligatory stop for tourists 'doing' the south of France, it has never been a place where we have wished to stay for long.

The canal going west from Aigues Mortes is without locks, long, undeviating and featureless, but a good deal more interesting than that might imply, not only due to the bird and animal life but because its route through flat salt marshes is unlike anything else experienced on French canals. It is a watery world, the canal itself often being nothing more than a dredged channel between narrow banks with salt water lakes on either side where shellfish of all kinds flourish, providing a living for the fishermen working these waters. Brightly painted little fishing-boats are everywhere as are the fishermen's nets suspended from little derricks or lying in long, hoop supported tubes on the bank. Apart from the periodic groups of clustered cottages housing the fishermen, there are few settlements on this canal but far over to the south along the coast, one can occasionally see the vast new developments catering to the throngs pouring out of northern French cities during July and August in search of a few days on a crowded beach beside the sea.

At the west end of the canal, one comes to Frontignan, dominated by the towers and tanks of a giant oil refinery which spreads its odious vapours throughout the town. One is often forced to spend longer than one would like in this blighted spot because of a road bridge, too low to go under, which opens only twice a day or while sitting out a blow on the Étang de Thau further west. The Étang is a shallow body of very salty water, separated from the sea by a narrow strip of sand, linking the Canal Rhône à Sète to the Canal du Midi. Only about thirteen miles long by three wide, it takes a little over an hour to cross in good conditions. But those conditions are significant on the Étang where high winds can kick up nasty waves in the shallow water and poor visibility can create navigational problems. If one strays too far from the navigable channel one can encounter very shallow water even half a mile from the southern shore, the hazard on the other side being long regimented ranks of oyster and mussel frames extending almost to the middle of the Étang. I recall the shock, once crossing the Étang de Thau, when I saw a man standing not a hundred yards from the boat with water only up to his knees!

The weather was kind for our passage of the Étang and on a windless, sunny day we entered the Canal du Midi at Les Onglous lighthouse. The Canal du Midi is a remarkable canal. Having been built in the seventeenth century it is not only one of the oldest but also the most ambitious of French canals, providing an inland link in partnership with the Garonne River between the Atlantic at Bordeaux and the Mediterranean at Sète. It was a tremendous undertaking for that time, carried out under royal warrant but conceived and executed by one remarkable man, Paul Riquet, Baron de Bonrepos, who did not live to see his brain-child finally reach completion in 1681. Such a canal had been talked about for many years but it was Riquet who solved the tricky problem of finding a reliable source of water for the canal and developed the system of feeder canals to bring the water to it. The Canal du Midi proper goes from the Étang de Thau to Toulouse where the now canalised Garonne takes over to complete the waterway to the west. Nearly all the locks east of Toulouse, over a hundred of them, are the original stone constructions with outward curving walls adopted for the canal, and many of the lockhouses and arched bridges are from the same period. At the time of its construction 45,000 plane trees were planted three to four yards apart on both sides of the canal to reinforce the banks and provide shade. It has also been claimed that these trees had the additional purpose of reducing evaporation of the canal water by the hot southern sun. Although the canal goes through terrain that is often hilly, the number of locks is kept low because it follows topographical contours rather than charging up and down hills as some canals do. The contour approach not only reduces locks but also produces a canal that twists and turns pleasantly with the hills and, in one place, results in a surprisingly long pound of thirty-two miles even as it traverses rolling countryside.

The Canal du Midi is no longer much used by commercial barges.

There are now only three or four left whose sole work is carrying wine from the prolific Languedoc vineyards to Bordeaux for mixing with the wine of that region. These barges are thirty metres or just under a hundred feet long, the maximum length for the Midi locks which are too small for the standard working French barges of thirty-eight and a half metres. Although a few locks at the eastern end have been lengthened to take them, modification of the entire canal is a long way off, if indeed it will ever happen. In the meantime, another kind of traffic is taking over the canal, drawn by its attractions and the long cruising season in the south. The number and size of companies hiring boats on the Canal du Midi has increased greatly in the past few years and seems to go on growing unchecked and uncontrolled. In the warmer months the canal is already so crowded with these boats that I fear many more will seriously affect the enjoyment of this marvellous waterway.

As *Lionel* slipped down the canal towards Agde, Pheasant's-eye Narcissus dotted the banks but the bare branches of the plane trees, being late starters, showed no sign of new green growth. There was certainly no spring joy in the heart of the lock-keeper at Agde's 'round' lock who grudgingly opened the gate for us after complaining of our use of the boat's horn to announce our presence. This lock, originally round, has three gates, two for the canal and a third for boats going to or from the branch canal connecting to the Hérault River on which the town of Agde sits. The roundness of the lock has, unfortunately, been destroyed by recent modifications to make mooring easier for hire boats which flock through it in the summer.

The town of Agde, about half a mile away and established as a settlement by Greeks 2,500 years ago, serves today as a simple market town for the local wine-growing district with few buildings of interest other than the forbidding dark lava stone cathedral beside the Hérault. On the shore of the Mediterranean to the east Agde has a swinging, money-making satellite at Cap d'Agde where the affluent have summer condos, expensive yachts and where, it is reputed, one can join, if so inclined, 30,000 others in a mass, bare-bodied enjoyment of the southern sun.

The south gave us some of this sun but no warmth as we sailed down the Canal to Béziers, one of the largest cities of Languedoc and the scene in 1209 of probably the bloodiest episode ever recorded in French history. Crusading forces outside the walls demanded that two hundred supposed heretics thought to be in the town be handed over to them. The citizens refused and, having bravely engaged the crusaders, were routed in the subsequent battle. The crusaders then entered Béziers and slaughtered the entire population of 20,000 men, women and children. It is said about this horrible atrocity that when the leader of the crusaders was asked how to tell the heretics from the true believers, he had replied: 'Kill them all. God will know which is which.' After that shattering blow the city languished for centuries, only regaining prosperity again with the burgeoning nineteenth-century wine industry.

On the quay at Béziers we met many friends last seen in Beaucaire and now cruising on the Canal du Midi. Two of these, a Dutch couple, were already on their way home with a smashed wheelhouse after an encounter with a bridge further west. The bridges of the Canal du Midi have a well-earned notoriety. Many are ancient stone affairs with round or elliptical arches adding much to the charm of this canal but their narrowness exacts a corresponding penalty, the curving arch fast reducing the clear height as one moves away from its centre. They must always be tackled with great care for a wrong approach or a determined puff of wind at a crucial moment can result in a damaging crunch. Our friend reported such a gust as his barge was about to pass through a bridge, swinging the stern away from the centre line. The wheelhouse was demolished by the impact with the bridge, leaving our friends bruised and bleeding in a shambles of shattered glass and splintered wood with their much-cherished old bronze bell lost for ever in the mud of the canal bottom. This grim lesson was not lost on me.

Although the beauty of the Canal du Midi in early spring had partly muffled my nagging worries about electricity, they wouldn't go away entirely. With the main generator dead, our sole source of electrical power was the tiny Honda, a gutsy little machine but showing signs of strain. To give us more security we therefore bought another, larger Honda and I felt a lot easier in my mind. The starter motor of the big generator was still sitting in Monsieur Laurent's untidy garage at Tarascon waiting for parts from the Spanish manufacturer, which I was told would take three weeks to arrive. At the time this seemed like a ridiculously long period but in the light of later events it appeared to have been even rashly optimistic.

In Europe, machines are often built with components from different countries. The generator, though far from complex, represented no less than three: France, Italy and Spain. The last was the homeland of the starter motor from where the parts to repair it seemed such reluctant emigrants. When I telephoned Laurent to discover what progress was being made, he reported encountering *un grand problème*. I might have known. That ubiquitous expression, now so familiar and so dreaded, came down the line like an electric shock.

Realising I could do little by phone, I went to Tarascon to sort things out in the incredible office of Laurent's equally incredible garage. There we both stood as he explained that the parts are first ordered from a Paris agency and, after a suitable lapse of time, are shipped from Spain, but to West Germany, not Paris, because the German industrial giant, Bosch, was then European distributor for all the Spanish company's products. From West Germany the parts would be shipped to the Paris agency and, finally, to Laurent, the little guy at the end of the line. I found it hard to believe and thinking there must be a faster way, I suggested to Laurent, standing by the phone in his peaked seaman's cap, that he should call the Paris agent of the Italian company that had made the generator's diesel motor. I gave him the number and he set about making the call on a telephone that seemed in the final stages of mechanical collapse. He fiddled with it, using his ballpoint pen but, at last, in exasperation began to take the thing apart, getting the plastic cover off and, along with it, of course, the numbers he needed for dialling. He then made several phone calls to unknown places, all by counting backwards to get the right finger holes but, getting fed up with this, finally wrote the numbers on the remains of the machine with a thick marking pen. After several more failed attempts to reach Paris, he called the telephone company in a fit of pique to complain about the telephone he had just dismembered all by himself. At this point I left the office for twenty minutes. On my return he called again, made contact, ordered the parts and obtained a promise of prompt delivery. He turned to me as he put down the phone, saying in the only English I'd ever heard him use: 'Very good'. I thought it was 'very good' too and that the starter motor was well on the way to being repaired. How wrong I was.

We soon left Béziers to continue west up the seven-lock staircase of Fonserannes and into the thirty-two-mile-long pound. Ascending the locks takes time as each chamber is filled in turn before the boat can move into the next one. Because of this a new *pente d'eau* or water slope has been built near the existing locks to speed the raising and lowering of boats. The *pente d'eau* consists of a concrete channel stretching from top to bottom of the hill and a large machine that raises or lowers a wedge of water including boats along the channel, the wedge being pushed by what amounts to a moving lockgate with rubber rollers against the concrete to stop water escaping. The propelling machine, a great monster of a thing, runs on massive rubber wheels along the sides of the concrete channel over which it towers.

A similar device has been in use for some time on the canal west of Toulouse but the one at Béziers, newer and different in design, has not been so successful. It operated for a while and then there was an 'incident'. On a rainy day with the wedge of water full of little hire boats, the whole kit and caboodle was on its way down when either the brakes failed or the rubber wheels skidded on the slick, wet concrete surface and the operators could not control it. Momentum picked up and the whole thing, machine, water and boats gathered speed as it swooshed to the bottom. The operators bailed out of the control cab, cracking bones as they jumped but the people in the boats were luckier, none, surprisingly, being hurt. As the whole ungainly business reached the bottom, it is reported that the water in the wedge sloshed over the gate at the lower end, forming a wave that travelled a mile down the canal to the next lock where it jumped the gate and carried on into the port of Béziers causing some damage to the moored boats there. Since that time, the huge machine has remained for many months motionless, its wheels jacked up in the air, waiting for someone to come up with the solution to its own *grand problème*.

The little village of Poilhes nestling on the side of a hill west of Béziers was to be our mooring for the next weeks during which I returned to Canada for ten days, leaving Melodie and Joss on the boat with friends close at hand. It is an attractive village, a particular favourite of ours, with inevitable though modest Roman legacies as proudly touted in its full name, Poilhes la Romaine. It is a tiny village island sitting in a rolling sea of vines accessible only by small back roads and the canal, running there along the side of a hill, offering splendid views of the valley below, the distant hills and, on exceptional days, the snow-capped Pyrénées.

Because Poilhes is only seven miles from Béziers it is not quite a simple country village, having acquired over the years a few affluent residents and, more recently, an expensive restaurant. But, for all that, Poilhes still retains its village charm and a population actively working the vineyards around it. Unlike so many canal villages, Poilhes, under the leadership of a progressive mayor, has exploited its canal location with a good quay and services people in boats need. For this reason and its sleepy attractions the village has become a cherished mooring place for the few who have discovered it. Although space on the quay was limited by the presence of two hotel barges laid up for the winter we managed to squeeze in at the extreme end of the line near an English motor-cruiser whose owner leapt suddenly into our lives a few days later.

It was three-thirty in the morning when Melodie heard a faint voice calling our names in the still night air. I was sound asleep and heard nothing but Melodie had her window open and that was lucky. Rushing out with a flashlight she asked if something was wrong. 'Yes,' said a voice from the darkness, 'there's a lady in the water'. Melodie, to whom the proper gear is always essential, came back to our boat for rubber-boots and warm clothing for it was bitterly cold outside. Why she didn't wake me I shall never know, but at last properly clothed, she rushed back to our new friend's boat to find him standing practically naked on the quay in socks and shorts holding the hand of a woman up to her neck in the frigid water of the canal. Because the water was over six feet deep, the quay high above the water and its wall vertical, there was absolutely no way the woman could get out. In addition she was fat and not only blue with cold but clearly drunk.

Things did not look promising. Our friend had already failed to pull her out and even with Melodie helping their efforts came to nothing. At that moment Melodie went off in a futile search for help but, strangely, once again neglected to call her husband who was still sleeping through the whole drama. When she returned, they tried again, each taking one of the woman's arms, and with a final yank managed to pull the sodden mass of almost lifeless female flesh up on to the quay. There she lay on the cold stones, faintly lit by the flashlight, a sprawled figure wearing boots, no skirt, shredded panty hose, torn blouse and blonde wig. Who was she? Where had she come from? How did she get into the water? Although these and other interesting questions danced through Melodie's head they remained unasked. But the bedraggled figure at their feet at least acquired a name. She was, it seemed, Colette.

While they were both considering what they were going to do with Colette it became clear to Melodie, as it had not before, that our friend more than matched Colette's condition in one important respect as he danced around, finding more merriment than Melodie in the predicament they faced. But Colette was finally stood on her rubbery legs and moved into our friend's boat. The poor woman was chilled to the core so they removed what remained of her wet clothes and the

equally wet wig, revealing a surprisingly brilliant head of red hair tied up in little pin curls, and finally put her into bed with a hot drink.

Colette was in a bad way; colder than she'd ever been before, drunk, badly grazed by the quay wall, clothing torn or lost, in a strange bed on a strange boat belonging to a strange man and a long way from home wherever that was. The next morning Melodie found the patient sitting on the bed crying and repeating over and over: 'What will my husband think?' Although this seemed like a pretty fair question to Melodie, she didn't pursue it, but helped Colette put on some of her own dry clothes. A very subdued and hungover Colette turned up at our boat later to get warm, shortly kissing Melodie and our friend goodbye and departed in her own car for home where an irate husband probably awaited her.

After the night-time caper we moved along to Capestang, the village that boasts the nastiest bridge to be found on the entire canal. It is low, it is narrow and it has an awkward-looking arch built of ugly, rough stone carrying the multi-coloured scars of earlier engagements with boats of every kind. If bridges had auras, the aura of the Capestang bridge would be an angry, flaming red and I was not at all sure that the mean-looking thing would allow *Lionel* to pass with the wheelhouse up. It had already nearly stopped our friends in the *Amity Belle* with a wheelhouse as high but wider than ours. In a desperate gambit they had filled their stern mounted dinghy with water to the gunwales and persuaded twenty-odd locals to come aboard for the short passage, hoping the additional weight would lower the boat enough to get through. These measures, alas, were not quite enough. The *Amity Belle* stuck under the bridge. Realising it was now or never, our friend Johnny simply powered the boat through, scraping stone from the arch which now bears, along with all the other marks, new ones left by the *Amity Belle*. But that would not work for *Lionel* and its more fragile demountable wheelhouse.

I approached our nemesis on the centre line at the slowest possible speed with Melodie stationed to push the boat one way or the other as required. Because you can't steer a boat at almost zero speed we wandered slightly off-centre. Although there appeared to be clearance to get through, Melodie felt she couldn't hold the boat to the centre by herself and we reluctantly backed away from the bridge and moored. A day or so later we demounted the wheelhouse and passed through the bridge. But putting the wheelhouse back together again was a wholly different matter. Because neither Melodie nor I is strong, tall or young, the effort left us completely whacked. It was not only the physical energy, agility and patience required that wore us down but all the nagging dimensional discrepancies that had to be solved along the way. It was all dreadfully depressing for me to have this first close look at the truly awful workmanship of the wheelhouse which I was now determined to have properly rebuilt. It was not one of the good days but there was some recompense for Melodie, at least, when our remorseful friend from Poilhes brought an enormous bunch of dried flowers to thank her for helping with his sodden night-time visitor.

Although Capestang is the worst, none of the canal's arched bridges can be treated casually, especially if one's boat has a high wheelhouse. And when these bridges occur, as they often do, at the entrance to locks, one must be doubly careful because of unpredictable currents from the lock sluices. At such a lock I misinterpreted a signal from Melodie and thinking she meant 'Stop!', I put the boat hard in reverse, immediately making matters worse. The stern rose slightly and a corner of the wheelhouse hit the arch, causing a shower of stone chips to clatter on to the deck but surprisingly, because of the wheelhouse's flexible construction, it absorbed the shock. While going into reverse may raise the stern of a boat, it is far more useful to know that pushing the throttle of a barge forward can lower it as much as six inches. I have seen a barge at Auxerre slowly approach a bridge the captain found a little too low to get under. He then backed off and passed it successfully at full throttle. But this requires courage and familiarity with the behaviour of one's boat. I have used the technique to ensure good clearance but have never mustered the confidence and plain guts to resort to it in a nip and tuck situation where only a slight misjudgement can mean the total destruction of a costly wheelhouse.

April brought warm weather as we travelled westward between the ranks of closely spaced plane trees, at last bursting into leaf and, to Melodie's distraction, shedding their fuzzy, round seed balls on *Lionel*'s deck as we passed underneath. The birds were back from winter holidays further south, filling the air with song that came as a surprise after the long winter silence. They flashed here and there through the branches on their busy spring routines and even the shy hoopoe could occasionally be seen among the trees with extended crest and flashing black and white wings. Poppies, basil, thyme, bitter vetch, wood spurge, herb robert, wild angelica and others splashed the arid vineyards with welcome colour as spring finally came to the Midi.

And spring had brought out hire boats in droves, their numbers greatly swollen by spring school holidays. Manned by eager but unskilled crews, plastic boats weaved back and forth down the canal, choked the locks and invaded the quiet mooring places one had selected with such care. One simply had to endure this brief spring madness although, at times, to avoid the crowd in the next few locks, we'd get underway at dawn to cruise all by ourselves past the sleeping boats. It is easy to become a little superior about hire boats and their crews but Melodie and I have always known how much we owe to the boats we hired for so many years. It was the way it all began for us. Hire boats were our teachers and hooked us on the water life. We now are members of a different group with our own converted barge, a group that tends to view with slight disdain the beginners in their plastic boats: 'tupperware' or 'noddy boats', as they are often called, even having a derogatory twist. Among private barge people, Anglo-Saxons especially, these words have become part of the jargon, a human and harmless enough little arrogance that hurts no one and reflects the typical attitude of the experienced towards those who are not. And

107

most of those on holiday in these boats certainly do lack basic boating skills. That is not their fault and it is also true that most of the boats they must learn to run in a matter of hours are not easy to handle, being light, steered from the front end and with a shallow draft that makes them intractable in a wind. But, for all their shortcomings, such boats have been the means for hundreds to discover and briefly enjoy the pleasures of a waterborne life as they were for Melodie and me. That is justification enough for a little tolerance.

Sweet spring

As spring took hold of the land, the ever-present vines, in endless parallel rows, sprouted leaves, clothing the dry hills on either side of the canal. Through this fast greening landscape we travelled to Carcassonne, the westerly limit of that year's cruise. Of all the places along the Canal du Midi, Carcassonne is easily the star attraction, its mediaeval fortress, la Cité, on a hill above the river Aude being one of the great sights of France and a powerful tourist magnet. It certainly deserves to be. As we approached Carcassonne along the canal the magnificent fortified town briefly showed itself sitting on its hill in the hazy distance. But the tourist buses soon bring one down to earth. Even in the winter months they debouch sightseers by the hundreds to swarm over this ancient place. Although they have tarnished the pleasures of the intricate old stone artefact it survives in spite of them and, strangely, it doesn't seem to matter too much. La Cité is old enough, big enough and certainly strong enough to master the temporary nuisance.

La Cité is claimed to be the largest fortress in Europe and it may well be but size isn't the main point about Carcassonne. La Cité appeals to most people, I think, because it matches their idea of what a mediaeval fortress should be; it conforms to their fantasies. With its turrets, steeply pitched roofs and castellated walls it could be lifted right off the page of some illuminated manuscript. And when seen on its hill, it is all too easy to complete the obvious mental image with life; the armoured knights, the horses, the colourful, flapping banners, the spear-bearing men. It is the very stuff of romance, a Camelot in real stone. On our final night in Carcassonne we dined with two Canadian friends within the walls of la Cité and walked back to the boat down the long hill in the dark with the floodlit walls and turrets hanging above us, dreamlike in the night sky. Even with the tourists it is still a magical place.

Our Canadian friends had come to join us for the return journey down the canal toward the east. Elizabeth and Ian had limited experience of boats and none of barges or French canal locks but they were enthusiastic about the coming cruise and eager to do their bit. We explained as fully as possible the locking procedure with its attendant hazards and off we went. On the eastward journey we would be descending in each lock. Since there would be no turbulence only one rope, on the midship bollard, would be needed for mooring. It all seemed simple enough but then, in the very first lock, the unexpected happened.

The locks on the canal are old with cracks between some of the lockside stones. As the boat slowly lowered in the lock, a rope being handled by one of our friends became stuck in such a crack. As the boat started to list I saw Ian vainly struggling to free the rope, but by then the boat was properly 'hung up' and only one thing remained to be done. Luckily there was a hatchet near me in the wheelhouse so I rushed out and cut the rope, a new nylon one, alas, with a loop recently spliced to its severed end. It was a nasty introduction to the canal for our poor friend who seemed much subdued by the experience and, later that day, sat a long time on the deck, trying hard to repair the rope with barely remembered Boy Scout splicing skills.

Recovering from the trauma of the first lock, we glided down the canal in warm sunshine filtering through new leaves on the canalside trees. There was no hurry so we stopped at whim to go for walks in the country now rich with wild flowers and the varied greens of spring. There were always places or things to investigate. We walked through the vineyards, explored old buildings, shopped in little villages and once, up a narrow feeder canal, discovered a delightful, hidden place where an old stone house, a dam, weirs with control gates all clustered together beside a sparkling stream, alive with trout. We read books sitting in the grass beside the canal, bought and ate asparagus fresh from a nearby garden, consumed much good food and drank a selection of the local wines. Life seemed good.

Far from being deterred by the crisis of the first lock, our friends continued to be active members of the crew, ever striving for that quiet competence I'm sure they yearned for. Standing at the wheel, I was a remote and sometimes amused observer of their work with ropes. They were so eager to do the right thing but understandably not sure how to go about it. I recall one lock when they were both ashore with a long rope as a kind of miniature mooring committee and uncertain about the next move. They must have reached a decision of sorts for, out of the corner of my eye, I saw them executing a mad, impromptu *pas de deux* along the side of the lock. As they both rushed to do something with the rope, they danced, tripped and pirouetted their way down the lock with the rope snaking under their feet. While watching them twisting and turning on their way to some as yet unfathomable conclusion, I sensed disagreement as to which to choose of the several options open (a common failing of committees). It was finally resolved and the comic ballet brought to an abrupt finale by Elizabeth's hasty retreat to adjust her slacks which threatened imminent collapse.

One of the pleasures of having friends aboard was to share with them the many things and places that we had so much enjoyed along the canal. The weather and the time of year combined to make our lazy journey east everything we could have wished for. We stopped briefly in Le Somail, the minute and charming canal village that was once the port for Narbonne and where the old canal structures still remain, including a fine arched stone bridge with a little seventeenth-century chapel used at one time by barge people. Surprisingly, Le Somail is also the place chosen by a Brest shipwright to build two large ocean-going schooners, incongruously sitting in the quiet canal, far from their proper element, fully rigged, masts reaching high above the village roofs. After Le Somail we had to face the Capestang bridge and once again demounted the wheelhouse, made so much easier this time with four pairs of hands. For the rest of that day we cruised along the sun-dappled canal with the wheelhouse down, the great new leaves of the plane trees just above our heads. It was a lovely experience, especially for the captain, normally cooped up inside and deprived of this rare open-air experience.

In Béziers, with the added mobility offered by the car, we made an excursion to the thirteenth-century Abbaye de Fontfroide tucked away in a remote valley of the Corbière hills west of Narbonne. No longer an active religious establishment, it is now in private hands, the home of three families who were responsible for its excellent restoration. The old Cistercian abbey, built of the warm Corbière stone, is a wonderful example of Romanesque architecture, but it is the atmosphere of the place that makes such an impression on the visitor. Set in a tranquil, isolated valley amongst cypresses and hills covered with yellow-flowering broom, it is far from the distractions and trivialities of modern life and transmits an all pervading feeling of peace and serenity that stays long in the memory.

On the same day we visited quite a different but also remarkable place, Oppidum d'Enserune, a hill beside the canal near Poilhes with ruins of a sixth-century Iberian/Greek city. It was, however, not for the ruins that we had come here but to look from the hill down on the remarkable *ancien étang* of Montady, a circular dish, about a mile in diameter, with wedge-shaped fields radiating from its centre. Originally a pond, it was drained for agricultural use by thirteenth-century monks, who built drainage ditches which now form the pie-shaped fields. The water is carried to the centre of the circle from where it flows underground to a nearby canal village which uses it for irrigation. It was a remarkable undertaking for that time and it was a remarkable sight in the spring with the odd-sized wedges bearing the variegated greens of different crops.

In those days Béziers was the home of a top-class *nouvelle cuisine* restaurant rating two stars in the red Michelin Guide. More recently it has lost its chef and its stars, making it hardly worth a visit, but then it was in high flight, justifying the large cost of a meal in its elegant dining room. It is in such two-star restaurants of France that Melodie and I look for our rare, extravagant treats, where the chef is often still young, working hard to excel at his job and, presumably, win a third star and all the riches that are bound to follow.

With unexpected ease I persuaded our friends that one of the costly but essential experiences of France was a meal in such a restaurant. Facing up to the financial truths of the evening we duly sat down at a table in the corner of the dining-room and examined the menu as we sipped our Kirs Royals. The *nouvelle cuisine* menu is usually a simpler thing than that of the traditional French restaurant and this followed the pattern, listing only two meals at different prices, each with nine or ten dishes. It was a simple choice and we all plumped for the cheaper of the two alternatives, which was certainly expensive enough. I then faced the daunting task of selecting wines from the vast choice available in the restaurant's cellar. Not being very good at this tricky business I tend, on such occasions, to point at moderately priced wines in the right categories and hope for the best. Unfortunately it doesn't always work, especially with white wines. After choosing one, the *sommelier* at my elbow gently asked if I wished to start the meal with such a sweet wine. Somewhat rattled by this, and realising that even my feeble pretence at connoisseurship had vanished, I blindly chose another white, dry, thank God, and a red as well. After the fumbled choice of wines we settled down to the main event. In my memory that meal has now become a pleasurable gastronomic blur, one delightful and beautifully arranged dish following another in an intriguing sequence, each a subtle and unusual combination of ingredients. What detail remains is fragmentary; thin strips of almost rare liver sitting on a nest of warm lamb's lettuce, a single huge, sliced scallop, the lightly fried yellow flower of a zucchini, the mid-meal pause for delicately flavoured *sorbets* made by the young chef. It was an exceptional meal; the food subtle, varied, often unfamiliar, always delicious but never excessive, the wine outstanding, the atmosphere elegant, the service impeccable and the bill horrendous.

With the departure of Elizabeth and Ian, we continued east along the canal to the Étang de Thau. There the wind was blowing hard, the last lock-keeper on the canal warning us not to attempt the crossing. But having had a closer look when we came to Les Onglous, I discovered that the waves were not excessive although the visibility was only just over half a mile, not great but good enough.

We crossed largely on a compass course, giving the shallow water on the south a wide berth, spray covering the boat many times, smacking the wheelhouse and drenching the flowers which Melodie had in tubs on the deck. (Only later did we find that the salt water had, alas, killed most of them.) After some confusion with marker buoys and a wrong turning we finally found the entrance to the Canal Rhône à Sète and headed down it for Aigues Mortes.

Not long afterwards we had to pass a loaded barge going in the opposite direction, normally no problem in this wide canal. But when we were abreast and the water level dropped, *Lionel* was seized as if by a giant hand and thrown against the bank. It happened so quickly I could do nothing but put the engine out of gear. The boat rebounded violently off the bank, returning to deeper water again once the barge had passed. I don't know what caused this strange behaviour and can only guess that the boat must have bounced off a bump in the mud on the canal bottom when the water was lowered by the barge's passing. It had never happened before nor has it since.

After a long day of running we spent the night in Aigues Mortes, treating ourselves to a simple but excellent meal of *crudités*, lamb chops and a *tarte aux poires* sitting beside a glowing fire at a restaurant just inside the walls of the town. We arrived in Beaucaire the following day to spend a week or two there before going back to Canada for the summer. Having decided that the troublesome wheelhouse must be rebuilt and its roof lowered, I made arrangements for this to be done by a retired Englishman living in the port on his own barge, beside which *Lionel* would be moored for the next few months. Although it seemed like a good arrangement there are always risks having work of this sort done in one's absence. However, I went over everything very carefully, did some drawings, prepared detailed instructions and, after that, could only hope for the best.

Béziers

We returned to Europe in 1984 to spend a year on *Lionel*. Beaucaire seemed much the same as before: the same industrial smells, the same wind, the same traffic swirling around the port and many of the same people. But *Lionel* had undergone a dramatic transformation. Even from a distance, the new wheelhouse came as a shock, its wood stained a strident reddish hue, and closer inspection revealed more that was at variance with my careful instructions of the spring before. The final blow was, of course, the bill, far beyond my most pessimistic guess. It was, as feared, the penalty absent owners must resignedly accept, but fortunately most of what was wrong could be later changed without great trouble. The new wheelhouse certainly was a vast improvement over the old one: lower, stronger, better built and more easily demountable. The builder had worked hard all summer to complete the job, doing, I knew, what he thought best. It was too late to complain about details so I said nothing and paid the carefully itemised bill.

The generator problems had not magically vanished over the summer months. I knew from correspondence that the incredible Monsieur Laurent of Tarascon still had not repaired the cursed starter motor even after four and a half months. In an attempt to expedite matters I had stopped, on the way south, to buy the parts from the agency which had promised to send them the previous spring and now claimed ignorance of the order, of any earlier correspondence, of either Laurent or even me. Finding that a whole new starter motor was only a hundred francs more expensive than the two parts needed, I bought one, brought it to Beaucaire and installed it myself.

Because I am a novice in the electrical mysteries, I asked Laurent to do the wiring and returned with him to his office afterwards where I paid his bill and recovered what was left of the old starter motor. Monsieur Laurent then sprung his surprise, producing statements which, to my utter astonishment, showed that the parts had actually been delivered to him some time before! If that were not enough, he calmly said, as if it were not at all unusual, that he had sent them back to Paris because they were too expensive! 'They are mad in Paris,' he said. It took me a while to absorb the full impact of this. After all that time and all those letters and the phone calls and the cost of the new starter motor, he had sent the parts back! In a calmer moment I reflected that Laurent, in spite of the apparent madness of what he'd done, was simply following the instincts of a good, money-conscious Frenchman in trying to protect me from what were, in truth, wildly excessive charges. When it was all over I felt a tinge of regret that Laurent and I would no longer have any more of those strange meetings in his cluttered office. Sadly, the chequered story of the generator would now have to stumble along without him.

Having wound up matters in Beaucaire, we finally left the town for the last time on a warm, sunny day at the end of September. For the next two days the Mistral was in full charge of things and our mooring at Aigues Mortes was the best place to be until it calmed down, neither the Étang de Thau nor the Canal Rhône à Sète being nice places in a strong blow. We arrived in Béziers a few days later intending to sit out the November closure of the Canal du Midi at Poilhes further west but as events unfolded the port of Béziers was to be our base for the next three months.

It was not a bad place to be: no beauty spot but relatively quiet, free of bothersome traffic and not far from the centre of the city. We were moored across the road from warehouses supplying local winegrowers with chemicals of all kinds and, not long after our arrival, noticed that one of these warehouses was attracting the attentions of officials who arrived in cars with Paris licence plates. Naturally curious, we discovered that the flap was because this warehouse contained large vats of the same chemical that had taken such a dreadful toll not long before at Bhopal in India. All during our long stay in Béziers we eyed the warehouse nervously and tried, in vain, to put this sword of Damocles out of our minds.

The other side of the basin had a totally different character with a row of old houses scattered along a little-used road, separated from the water by a magnificent line of mature plane trees then bare of leaves. These trees marched down the bank in close formation, defining with great elegance the morning mists and pink evening skies, their reflections in still water creating a spectacular double image. When one looked in their direction, the mooring basin even seemed a beautiful place.

The port of Béziers that autumn had a mixed and shifting population of people from England, Hawaii, Denmark, Germany, Holland and France living on boats as varied as their owners. At one end of the scale were the yachts of the French contingent, a sleek sailing machine and a large motor-cruiser. And then there were Maggie and John, a young English couple living on a small owner-built catamaran, the *Maiden UK*, with what must surely have been the bare minimum of living space. These two soldiered on in increasingly trying conditions as winter advanced but never complained unduly about their icy boat. They became good friends of ours as did the two young Dutchmen living in a state of high domestic disorder on a tiny and decrepit barge they shared with a dog, some chickens and a goat.

While the domestic animals gave the two Dutchmen eggs and milk, these were not enough in themselves. They expanded their diet by foraging in the deserted vegetable gardens on the outskirts of the town and, more profitably, behind the local supermarket where they struck an unexpected mother lode in the trays of food discarded because it had passed the date before which it should be eaten. It was in all respects perfectly good food, not contaminated by other garbage, only a shade past its prime and a bonanza for Willi and Diemer who had so little money to spend. The only catch was that these feasts might be all buns one day and all fruit tarts the next, a monstrously ill-balanced food intake but, if you're young, hungry and penniless, the niceties of nutrition count for very little. And, when you get right down to it, several meals of strawberry tarts is a marked improvement over no meals at all.

Willi and Diemer lived a vagabond existence, scrounging food wherever they could, working and washing as little as possible, dressing as casually as casual can get. Diemer, with confused curls of blond hair radiating like a grubby nimbus from his scalp and soiled, ill-fitting clothes hanging limply from a lean frame, was certainly on the wilder side of casual. One would never have thought that this scarecrow man could so ably undertake building a new roof for *Lionel*'s wheelhouse as he subsequently did.

Some of the last warm weather of that autumn tempted eight of us to go for a picnic in the hills near Minerve west of Capestang. The setting was outstanding, a remote height of land sparsely covered with gorse on the very edge of a precipice forming one side of the Canyon de la Cesse, a gorge three-hundred feet deep, cut by the little river through the rocky hills. We had our lunch of cheese, pâté, bread and wine sitting in the sun on the very lip of the gorge, the two dogs, Joss and Diemer's Pica, wandering precariously around the picnic place. Immediately in front of us the rough face of the opposite cliff was pockmarked with caves, some of them occupied in the not too distant past by outlaws. All around us the gorse was interspersed with small vineyards of golden vines then heavy with grapes being picked in the annual *vendange*. Beyond, a rolling sea of hills dropped away in great purple-tinged swells, fading to pale blue in the far distance. It was a wonderful place. I would have been quite happy sitting there all afternoon but the more energetic members of the picnic yearned to visit a prehistoric cave two hundred feet below and off we set, slipping and partly falling down a precipitous path, so steep in places we had to climb down chimneys hanging on to cables set in the rock face. The cave proved to be a disappointment so we retraced our weary steps up the cliff, arriving out of breath at the top, Melodie's hand gashed and bleeding from the steel cable. We then all retired to sip coffee in the shaded forecourt of a café in Minerve, a little village where long ago a hundred and eighty heretic Cathards were burnt to death by yet more bloodthirsty crusaders.

Ever since leaving Beaucaire the large generator had remained silent and unused. Thinking it was time to bring it back to life, I asked an Englishman who ran a small hire-boat company in the port and, by repute, a good mechanic, to look the generator over. Down in the engine-room he fiddled around a bit and then asked me to start it. I did this and immediately poked my head down the hatch to see how things were going. What I saw in the gloom of the engine-room was a brilliant fan-shaped burst of sparks spewing like fireworks from where the starter motor lived. It was an eye-catching display but the gut-wrenching noise accompanying it sounded like, and was, the death throes of fast-moving machinery bent on violent suicide. Simultaneously we rushed to turn everything off but it was too late: the damage had been done.

We stared at the generator in stunned silence for several long moments. Then the brand-new starter motor was removed, revealing its drive cogs cruelly ground down in a few seconds to useless stumps and its motor winding mangled beyond repair. How could this have happened? It happened, alas, because the motor had been installed incorrectly by none other than the captain himself, the latest in a long line of inept mechanics. It was a humbling moment. But by cannibalising the old starter motor we managed to get one in working shape. This was installed and there matters rested for the moment.

Since arriving in Béziers we'd noticed that a section of the quay was painted with strange yellow stripes. We were uncertain about their meaning and had not given them much thought, mooring in the most convenient place, yellow stripes or not. On the Canal du Midi, apart from barges carrying wine, there are one or two school barges carrying children for a week or two at a time. One day such a barge came into the port and cruised very slowly down the quay close to our boat, the captain shouting something at us which I didn't understand. He then turned at the end of the basin and came back alongside *Lionel*, still yelling incomprehensibly. As I stared dumbfounded, he jumped aboard and untied our mooring lines. Back on his own boat, the master diplomat told his browbeaten wife to put the loop of a heavy barge rope over one of our bollards. By this time I was also shouting but it made no difference. The mad *marinier* simply pulled us back with his barge by brute force, cast us adrift and took our old mooring place, pushing us even further back with the wash from his screw. By then floating at right angles to the quay, we didn't have an easy time getting the boat properly moored again.

I suppose if I had been younger, bigger and more violent by nature, I might have reacted physically to this impudent bully but, in the heat of the moment and things being as they are, I couldn't even think of anything nasty to say in French. What this man did was certainly extraordinary if not illegal, even if we were moored in a place reserved for barges. I have since heard that the same neurotic gent did something yet more drastic in cutting the mooring lines of a hotel barge with an axe. If he is not yet in trouble with the authorities he surely soon will be.

The principal reason for our extended stay in Béziers that winter was the new roof for the wheelhouse. It had not been part of the reconstruction in Beaucaire and had shown grave inadequacies during the autumn's heavy rainstorms. Its replacement in Béziers was essential and the Englishman who had worked on the generator undertook to do the job. It got under way in fits and starts, its progress slowed by weather, errors and countless distractions. Concerned by this, I insisted that extra help be employed and Diemer, the young Dutchman, then joined the work force, shortly having to shoulder the entire burden when the 'prime contractor' fell off a scooter and broke his hand. Diemer had only rudimentary carpentry skills and little experience or knowledge of this craft but what he lacked in these he more than made up for in intelligence and, even more important, the right mental attitude for the work at hand. We owe much to him for the way he carried the work through to its completion, even denying himself a chance to go home for Christmas. He was a slow, careful worker and, in his own way, a perfectionist, at times tearing out and re-doing work he rightly judged not good enough. The final stage of applying a glass-fibre finish was, however, beyond him technically and we were fortunate to have the necessary knowledge in the person of a local lock-keeper who gave advice and, at critical moments, did the work himself. The panels were, at last, installed at the end of December and Diemer took off with his dog to spend New Year in Holland.

It was during this time that we came to know a *clochard* living on the quay not far from *Lionel*'s mooring. If you travel the country in a boat you are certain to come across many *clochards*: it may be that they are attracted to the scavenging opportunities that ports and canals present or the chance of shelter offered by derelict buildings or the vacant ground where fires can be made without fear of harassment, or perhaps all of these. But, whatever the reason, we have frequently found ourselves where there are also *clochards*. This has never been a worry because, for the most part, they live their own quite separate lives and do not interfere with those of others. Many of them are certainly alcoholics within the limits of what they can find to drink and not unfamiliar with the advantages of occasional petty theft but we have never felt any fear of them nor suffered from their presence. If anything it has been quite the opposite.

Pierre was a *clochard* of a rather different kind. He was a resident of the quay at Béziers, living near us in a shelter attached to one of the warehouses, for which he served with the proprietor's approval as a kind of watchman. He first came into our lives when Diemer borrowed our car to take him to hospital after breaking his ankle in a fight at a local football game. He was to be picked up from the hospital later but long before the appointed time he came stumping down the quay after dark in a walking cast, using a short plank as his only crutch. Pierre was clearly a man of very independent spirit. Although obviously in great pain, he didn't ask for help but we gave him nevertheless pills for the pain, food for strength and a bottle of wine for his flagging morale.

Pierre was a long time recovering, unable to fend for himself, go in search of food or even move much. Melodie was very concerned about him and each day for the next few weeks took him a hot meal, a bottle of wine and some bread. To begin with, the bread was always brown,

Melodie thinking it was better for him. But I eventually persuaded her that, to a Frenchman, brown bread was almost like no bread at all and she switched to the crusty white air-filled stuff the French eat in such vast quantities. Pierre's ankle finally healed and, fed up with the cast, he removed it himself, having lost patience with what he called 'fussy hospital rules'.

Pierre never took any of our help for granted, constantly expressing his gratitude to Melodie in many small ways, sometimes with flowers. Nor did he take advantage of his relationship with us, except on one occasion. On the special day when people take flowers to the cemeteries, Pierre wanted to visit a nearby town so he could put flowers on the grave of his seven-year-old son killed some time before in an accident. So we drove him to the cemetery where he placed a huge pot of chrysanthemums on his son's grave. We knew very little about Pierre and, as we were leaving the cemetery, I asked him if he still had any family living in the town. He replied: 'Yes, my wife and three other children but I never see them.' He then added: 'I'm the one wearing horns.' This baffled me at the time but later I discovered that his wife was living with another man and Pierre was, therefore, a cuckold. Other facts about Pierre gradually came to light. He had known some prosperity as a masonry contractor with twelve men in his employ, but he was a hot-tempered man and had lost his wife, his family, his business and even run foul of the law. His life had fallen apart and Pierre had retreated finally into the life of a *clochard*.

During our enforced stay in the port at Béziers, our little Renault had been a godsend. This moderately faithful but disreputable servant had bumped and rattled us over the back roads of Languedoc on many happy excursions but it was falling apart from rust and the time had come to say farewell. I therefore started my rounds of the used car lots. Finding a car was quite easy but, not surprisingly, there was little interest in the old Renault. I had offers that were nothing less than insulting, and one dealer who refused to take the car at all. But then I got lucky. Finding a car I wanted at a fair price, I sat down in the office of the dealer. He hadn't even bothered to look at the Renault, merely glancing at a book of used car prices. When he asked me how much I wanted for the car I was emboldened by his casual approach and mumbled unconvincingly a figure 2,000 francs above what I had hoped to get. He contemplated this for a moment and then, to my astonishment, agreed. The poor man could not have known what he was landing himself with but no matter, it was a good moment for one who has spent more than his fair share of time on the other side in such affairs.

Getting the car was, in some ways, easier than getting the licence for it, the *carte grise*. It is not a simple matter in France where most aspects of a Frenchman's life are entangled in an intricate bureaucratic warp and woof. Visitors to the country can fortunately avoid becoming enmeshed in the administrative system but one brushes up against it from time to time and getting a *carte grise* is one of them. That there are *carte grise* specialists who collect a fee for weaseling these precious documents out of the system is proof enough of the problem's existence. And for someone living on a boat that moves from place to place the problem appears insoluble without resorting to deception. It boils down to a matter of residence. If you don't have a permanent address you can't have a *carte grise*. So what do you do? You devise a trick to deceive the system. It is commonly done, even winked at by the bureaucrats, but it's a trick nevertheless, a typically Gallic fiddle to solve an apparently insoluble problem. You create a fictitious residence for the *carte grise* application by borrowing the address of a friend or acquaintance, including a copy of a recent electricity bill and possibly a letter saying you are a resident of the given address. This will usually satisfy the bureaucrats and you get your *carte grise*.

During that winter the port of Béziers had its resident population of beasts as well as humans. On board *Lionel* there was, of course, our own Dalmatian, Joss, much spotted, much loved and a little spoilt. She was a constant companion wherever we went, even in hotels and restaurants, France being the most dog-tolerant of European countries. Willi and Diemer, the young Dutchmen, shared their little barge with a border collie and what amounted to a mini farm whose maxi smell permeated every corner of their boat. It comprised a few chickens and their pride and joy, a black nanny goat. There were also, of course, a lot of dogs about, the commonest boat pet. They flitted in and out or led almost secret lives aboard their owners' boats but were for the most part bland, everyday types without personalities that made them stand out. This, however, was not true of Jamie, a little Scottie, who spent a few weeks on the quay. He was an exceptional little beast: affectionate but not mawkish, independent but no loner, gutsy without being rash, intelligent but often endearingly mad. Chasing balls was his addiction, dirty old yellow tennis balls, stolen or wheedled from the players on the nearby courts. One by one these would be lost in the water but Jamie's solution to the ball shortage was simple: he'd trot casually on to the tennis courts and, by cajolery or theft, return shortly with his mouth full of more yellow fuzz, ready to start his mad chasing back and forth all over again.

Pierre, the *clochard*, also had a pet, a duck he had won in a local fair by managing to throw a hoop around its neck. Pierre and the duck lived happily together in his shed but he was always concerned for its safety because of the other *clochards* living nearby who were no friends of his, and who probably had their eye on it for a forthcoming meal. On an equally sombre note, we often witnessed one of the realities of French life as it unfolded across the basin from *Lionel*. Rabbits and chickens were kept by one of the households there and often on a Sunday morning we'd see one of the unfortunates being carried to the canal bank where the doomed rabbit or chicken would be dispatched, then skinned or plucked and cleaned, the executioner returning to his house with the corpse, leaving bloody débris behind for later disposal by scavenging dogs.

Although reconstruction of the wheelhouse roof introduced its inevitable disruptions, Melodie managed, as always, to keep life aboard running smoothly in spite of everything. Amongst many other things she is a talented cook. We both enjoy good food but she is the producer and I am only a lucky consumer who has been lapping up her wonderful food for close to forty years. But there were many others, during those months in Béziers, who also benefited from Melodie's meals. Not only was she cooking for Pierre, who must have been surprised at the quality of his daily meal, but also for the countless visitors who came to *Lionel* at that time. All this meant long periods in the little kitchen for Melodie but it was never drudgery for her. She rejoices in her craft and specially in sharing it with others. Feeding our friends the best way she knew how gave her endless pleasure and her meals were frequently a revelation for them as well.

I'm not sure if the meals Melodie produced in Béziers were particularly good because of the marvellous raw materials to be found in the town's covered market but Béziers certainly provided another, perhaps even stronger attraction for her. With a huge basket in her hand she would disappear each Friday morning to visit the flower market in Allée Paul Riquet, the broad main street of the town. She would return hours later laden with great bunches and pots of flowers to add to *Lionel*'s already richly blossoming interior. There were flowers on the tables in the wheelhouse and the *salon*, on every available shelf, above the sink and the refrigerator. There were flowers in Melodie's cabin and sort of a herbaceous border on the broad shelf in front of the wheel. The glory of French horticulture had invaded the entire boat, except, that is, for the captain's few carefully defended pockets of male austerity.

While stationary in the port at Béziers over those months, concerns about electricity plagued my waking hours as usual. We were then depending heavily on the little Honda generators but even these reliable machines began to falter for no apparent reason. Theories abounded but the hard truth emerged when they were taken in for repairs. Some time before I had bought nine plastic jerricans to hold gasoline for the Hondas and a reserve of diesel fuel for the main engine. I suppose I should have known but I didn't. The gasoline had dissolved some of the plastic which had gummed up the workings of the little generators. After the essential but costly repairs, gasoline was stored in metal containers but foolishly I did nothing then about the jerricans holding diesel fuel. Not long after, the diesel fuel also went to work on the plastic and one day I found a small lake of the stuff where the jerricans were stored under the seats in the wheelhouse. All nine now useless jerricans had to be thrown away. Another lesson had been learnt and I began to wonder how many more of these expensive 'learning experiences' I must endure.

Midi winter

With the wheelhouse roof finished and the Canal du Midi open again there was no reason to stay in Béziers. Three months was long enough. In early January we went up the seven-lock staircase and down the long pound to Poilhes to leave *Lionel* there while we took a short break, briefly in Spain and then right across southern France into northern Italy. It was not a good time to choose. The worst winter conditions in forty years blanketed Europe with heavy snow and killing frosts. A foot of wet snow welcomed us in Nice where people were skiing in the streets. In Italy conditions were worse. Snow closed the autostrada, weighed down the palms in La Spezia and one morning in Piacenza the temperature was –17°F which is cold even in my own country. Conditions were not much better in the Midi where there was more than four inches of ice in the canal. Although a friend had kept some heaters going in *Lionel* there was still frost damage to a few pipes. But the devastation was severe throughout the south of France where no precautions are taken against this kind of thing. Nearly all the spiky cactus so typical of the Midi was killed that winter, afterwards lying flat on the ground like limp green stars. Many vegetable crops were ruined, fruit trees damaged, pipes burst and boats, by their hundreds, suffered grievous hurts to plumbing, pumps and engines.

By the time we returned to Poilhes the worst was over. Although still cold, the temperature didn't seem to deter the *chasseurs* roaming the vineyards all rigged out with hunting gear and the camouflage clothing they affect. The French are mad about *la chasse*. At weekends they were everywhere, singly or in pairs, with or without dogs, searching the lean countryside for something to shoot at. Although France isn't exactly crawling with game this doesn't seem to worry the macho *chasseur* who satisfies his atavistic urges by loosing off at anything that moves regardless of size, and it is perhaps due to these diligent hunters that one rarely sees any dead wild game on the roads of France, the *chasseurs* presumably having got to it first.

Around Poilhes, the bare winter vineyards offered them slim pickings and, during the very cold weather, hunting was stopped entirely by the authorities, in a move that didn't seem typical of French bureaucracy. There was no obvious reason for doing this except as a humane gesture towards the little beasts and birds, already having a tough enough time just surviving. And what good was that when the ban was lifted with the return of warm weather? But at least during the brief pause a blissful peace descended on the vineyards. Then the warm weather came and the ban was lifted. That first weekend, all hell broke loose. The countryside crawled with brave *chasseurs* scouring the vineyards, bent on slaughter, but the vines, bare of leaves, provided little cover, leaving only a few small birds and rodents. Even with bad marksmanship, however, little could have survived the weekend offensive. With lead-shot peppering the canal and even the boat itself, we gazed in wonder and disgust at these normally harmless men blasting into bloody oblivion the few living things left around us.

Leaving Poilhes, we travelled west down the canal towards Castelnaudary. Like all canals, the Midi has its own peculiarities. Many I was familiar with, having encountered them before, but I had forgotten about the strange currents at the downstream end of some locks which tended to throw the boat hard against the lock wall at the critical moment of entering it. I did my best to make the necessary corrections but the result always seemed to be the same and it was clear from paint marks on the stone that others had the same problem. Only later, by throwing bits of bark into the water, did I discover that the current from the lock sluices was exactly opposite to what one could reasonably expect and with this knowledge I could counteract its effects.

But the turbulence in the air was far less predictable as a strong, gusting wind dogged us for days on our ascent through the many locks to Castelnaudary. There was some shelter from it below the locks but, once on top, *Lionel* was exposed to the full blast, usually from the beam, forcing us up against one side or other of the lock and making departure difficult. Once the boat had been pushed out from the curving lock walls with all ropes and crew aboard, it was vital to get under way quickly before the wind took charge again. Regrettably this manoeuvre was not always carried out with consummate skill. I recall with pain the exit from one lock on a particularly windy day when, in my eagerness to get moving, I overdid the throttle, tried to correct my mistake with the rudder, and as we left the lock, hit one lock gate a glancing blow, then the other, the lock-mistress staring sourly after us as we hurried down the canal.

These windy days were a sore test for both of us but especially Melodie, who had to work harder and a damn sight faster in the locks. Mooring wherever possible on the windward side made the exit easier but it meant that Melodie must disembark quickly and secure both mooring lines before the wind blew the boat away from the lock wall. She had to be fast with the ropes, tying them with knots that would not slip. Her unique, personally devised knot was surprisingly effective but took too long to tie and untie so I persuaded her to learn the clove hitch, probably the fastest holding knot for a bollard. She did this reluctantly, but, after much practice, got it sorted out, coming finally to an acceptance of its clear advantages.

It was on this stretch of the canal that we evolved a new method of dropping Melodie off on the bank and picking her up again. Previously this was done by bringing the boat into the bank and stopping it in the mud and weeds at the edge of the canal. I then had to push it out with a boathook before I could get underway again, an operation that used up time and effort. We now found that if the boat approached the bank with some forward motion, it would glance off the bank and return to the deeper water, giving Melodie a moment at the point of tangency to jump off, or on. This was a rough and ready way of accomplishing what many commercial barges do by using booms about twenty feet long which can swing out on either side of the boat. The person going ashore simply leans on the boom and kicks off, the return trip needing someone on board to swing the boom to the person on shore. We had toyed with the idea of fitting *Lionel* with such booms but they clutter the deck and, for us, are hardly as necessary as they might be for a loaded barge unable to come close to the canal bank.

After the final staircase of locks at Castelnaudary, we entered the *Grand Bassin*, a broad expanse of water with the town mounting a slope on the far side. Castelnaudary owes much to the Canal du Midi, having been an important place for the commercial traffic it once carried and a stopover for passenger boats travelling on the canal in the old days. This has all gone but, in a different way, the large British hire-boat company based here keeps alive the town's commercial ties with the canal. Castelnaudary is also the mainland headquarters of the French Foreign Legion, but perhaps its principal claim to fame is *cassoulet*, the stew of white kidney beans, sausages and *confit* of goose that is touted everywhere, even sold to tourists in cans. It comes in many forms with different meats and secret ingredients but the beans are as constant as the competing claims to be its true home. It doesn't seem to be a dish worth fighting over but most agree that Castelnaudary's claim to be the *cassoulet* capital of France is probably valid. I, for one, am quite content to let them keep it and the *cassoulet* as well.

We didn't take *Lionel* further west but Castelnaudary was a good jumping-off place for excursions by car so we locked the boat and went away with Joss, first to Bordeaux and Périgord and then later, on a separate trip, into the Pyrénées. But we never left the boat for long, enjoying too much our tranquil mooring on the canal with little going on but the long wriggling trains of ducks cruising back and forth, intent on important business of their own. It was a peaceful place and a peaceful time of year, with hardly a boat to disturb the calm of the canal in winter. But being winter, it was often cold and we counted on our central heating. Then one morning, the furnace refused to start.

Well, I thought, here we go again. I found a heating specialist, a Spaniard who had come to France with his refugee parents at the time of the civil war. He was a nice fellow, speaking a French sounding so much like Spanish that communication between us hung on a very slender thread. But he knew his job and soon found the trouble to be a faulty photo-electric cell, the replacement for which, he said, was not available locally and 'would have to be sent from the north by mail'. I sensed something awfully familiar in this and waited expectantly for what would certainly follow. Sure enough, after two days, when I called at the man's house to find out what was going on, his wife reported in staccato Spanish/French: '*Il y a un problème*'. Oh God, I thought, not again! The horribly familiar words were ringing in my ears as I returned to the boat, fearing the worst. It was shortly confirmed by the heating man who said he had telephoned Toulouse, Lyon, Bordeaux and even driven to Carcassonne to locate the part but without success. The problem, he said, was that the oil burner had been made in ITALY! Another cruel and terribly familiar twist of fate! The manufacturers had, he said, changed the design and the part, regrettably, was no longer available. So what was to be done? The only way to get the furnace working again was to buy a brand-new burner. So the costly thing was installed and the old one joined the fast-gathering cargo of defective equipment lying lifeless below in dark recesses of the engine-room. It was a sad business but even this ill wind blew a little lesson my way in the form of information which may help me side-step such trip-wires in the future. The good heating man told me that, in France, it is always prudent to buy equipment bearing the letters NF standing for *Norme Française* which implies conformity to certain standards and availability of parts. Was it really true?

In early March, we retraced our steps to the east, travelling most of the way in company with a friend, in his own boat. Stewart was in a hurry, setting a sizzling pace down the canal greatly in excess of even the most generous interpretation of the authorised speed limit and we whipped through the locks with the ease that extra hands made possible. But the old adversary, a strong, gusting wind, was a constant travelling companion, creating the usual surprises and predicaments. Because the effects of such a wind can be sudden and sometimes damaging, it is handy to know from which direction it is blowing. Approaching each lock I carefully scanned the water, the trees, chimney smoke, hanging laundry and *Lionel's* own flag for clues about the wind before deciding which side of the lock to moor on. But it was true on this journey, at any rate, that what held for the wind on the canal did not apply to the lock because of the effect of buildings, trees and terrain. Often enough, what seemed to be a steady wind from one direction on the canal turned into something entirely different at the lock. So willy-nilly, regardless of canal conventions, the lock-keeper's strong wishes and Melodie's careful deck arrangements, she had to hustle to prepare the ropes and herself for docking on the other side.

These last-minute scrambles were regrettable but if I have learnt anything about wind it is that, whenever possible, going with it rather than fighting it puts far less strain on both boat and crew. Melodie became quite proficient at these frantic last-minute changes, seeming able to jump further and quicker than before, having devised a kind of Zen approach to the business by putting herself mentally where her feet were to land. Then she leapt, keeping her feet together and, if necessary, rolling forward on to her knees and hands in a kind of rubbery parachute-jumper's technique. It isn't quite how I would do it but her legs are not the same as mine. It certainly appeared to work for her, although doing this kind of thing often on hard, uneven surfaces can begin to tell when you are over sixty.

As we went east, the plane trees lining both banks were still bare of leaves and submitting to their annual pruning by the canal authorities. I am not sure why they do this nor why they do it so drastically nor how the trees can possibly survive such fearful amputations. The plane tree, allowed to grow normally, has a sturdy dappled trunk with branches spreading out eight to ten feet above the ground to form the crown. It is common, however, in some sections of the canal to see all these branches cut off four feet from the trunk. The tree somehow continues to grow, putting out small shoots from the stumps but will give little shade in the hot months to come. Even more drastic surgery was evident in one part of the canal where no branches were left at all, the trunks having been cut off square below them. The canal there looked totally denuded, lined with nothing but the barren trunks, making further growth and shade extremely doubtful.

We moored at Poilhes briefly on our way east and on a cold day witnessed again the danger that lies so close to the towpath. A little boy being taken for a walk by his grandfather fell off the quay into the icy water. The quay wall was so high that the man could not get the boy out and had to jump in himself. The water was too deep for him and I doubted he could swim. As we came running, he managed to push the boy up far enough for me to get a grip on the seat of his pants and pull him on to the quay. But the grandfather was another matter. He was only just managing to keep afloat by scrabbling at some projecting stones but was too heavy for Melodie and me to lift. Fortunately some men soon came from a nearby house and hauled him out, very wet and badly frightened. Our friend Gordon had a similar experience when a railing gave way on his boat and he fell into a canal in heavy winter clothing. He could not climb back on his boat nor up the canal bank and probably would have drowned but for a woman on a nearby barge who heard the splash as he fell and summoned help.

By the end of March spring was well advanced. The almond blossom, always the first to appear, had gone by then to be replaced by cherry blossom and, soon after, apple. But the weather still alternated erratically between winter's chill and the warm promise of summer. Although the sun shone out of a blue sky as we returned to Béziers, the Mistral was again blowing from the north, giving the port an unpleasant, restless feeling, thankfully balanced by the warm welcome of friends.

At Béziers, Pierre the *clochard* was still living on the quay, but in rather different quarters. What few possessions he had, including his beloved duck, had been stolen. He blamed the other *clochards* with whom he had never been on good terms and had taken steps to prevent further theft by occupying a far more secure but unusual shelter, supposedly a secret. A friend of his, working in one of the warehouses, had whispered something to me about a *bascule* but I was busy at the time and didn't look the word up in my dictionary. Only later did I realise that he was referring to the warehouse's truck scales as Pierre's new place of residence. It was an odd choice but an ingenious one. The concrete chamber below ground and its steel platform above gave shelter from wind and rain, would be cool on hot summer days and would be safe from intruders since the only access was through a lockable steel trap-door. Before we left Béziers he turned up to say goodbye bringing flowers for Melodie and a bottle of wine for me. I

131

was greatly relieved not to see the cage of canaries he had talked about giving Melodie a few days earlier. Although I had done my best to deflect him from that idea, you could never be sure about the quixotic Pierre.

In the middle of April both boat and car were moved to Agde where we stayed a week, during which I took the car further on to Beaucaire making it easier to retrieve later from Lyon. While in Beaucaire I visited the nearby Rhône lock, then empty and undergoing repairs but confirmed there that the *chômage* would be over shortly. The way was now clear for our long journey north and I returned to Agde to make the final preparations.

Trouble with the *patron*

I am a mild-mannered man, not the kind who seeks confrontations in restaurants and would, indeed, go to some length to avoid them. But there always comes a time when enough is enough and a stand must be made. Such an occasion occurred when Melodie and I were travelling near Bordeaux on an excursion from Castelnaudary. We had entered a small town on a Sunday just after mid-day. There was only one restaurant open, small, a little run-down but marginally acceptable. Leaving Joss in the car, we walked through the bar and found a table in the crowded dining-room behind – crowded more, I would guess, because it was the only place open than for the quality of its cuisine. We ordered our meal, such as it was: *hors d'oeuvre* for Melodie, chicken, *haricots verts* and *pommes frites* for us both, wine for her, beer for me. After a few minutes the *hors d'oeuvre* and drinks arrived with a watery soup that I had not ordered. Melodie finished her dish of odds and ends, I toyed with my soup, we sipped our drinks. We waited patiently as three-quarters of an hour went by, bringing no sign of more food. My patience began to wear thin. The problem didn't seem to lie with the one overworked waitress serving all the tables but in the kitchen itself where we had glimpses through the swinging doors of someone shuffling around watching television and, I suppose, occasionally cooking. After an hour even patient Melodie thought the delay unreasonable and I started making 'get on with it' signs to the waitress. By this time we were ravenous, looking forward greedily to the *pommes frites*, a rare treat for us. After an hour and ten minutes had passed our main course arrived at the table but without the yearned-for *pommes frites*. Pointing out this significant omission, I was told the supply had run out. That was the last straw and I asked for the bill. It was for the price of the entire meal, ignoring the fact that our food came seventy minutes late, lacked important elements and had not been eaten. I refused to pay the bill as presented but left on the table generous compensation for what we had consumed, informed the *patron* of my intention and walked out with him jabbering at our heels.

As we reached the car, the *patron* still behind us, I threw my raincoat on the back seat and tried to get Joss organised for our departure. Her attention diverted by this, Joss didn't react in her normal way to the stranger near the car, neither barking nor making a lunge at the open door. It was a pity, for it gave the *patron* the split second he needed to reach in and grab my raincoat, running back with it to the restaurant where he threw it on the floor behind the bar. Reasoning with such a man was pointless but he opened a way to a solution of the ridiculous business by threatening to call the police. I agreed willingly and heard him complaining over the phone about the dreadful client who refused to pay for his meal. I let that go and rejoined Melodie in the car to await the arrival of the *gendarme*. After another long wait no one appeared and thinking that something could be gained if the accused client went to the police himself, we drove to the police station where I presented the facts of the case. The *gendarme* seemed like a reasonable type although naturally reluctant to get involved in such a trivial matter. But he duly arrived at the restaurant, a nice man in a difficult position, unhappy at the thought of taking sides, but he did his job gallantly, hearing arguments from both parties with quiet patience.

A remarkable scene then ensued. The angry *patron* fumed and blustered behind the bar with all the exhibits of the case arranged in front of him: EXHIBIT 'A', our rejected chicken and *haricots verts* (now cold), EXHIBIT 'B', the bill submitted by the *patron*, EXHIBIT 'C', the plate bearing my coins. The *patron* opened the proceedings, greatly distorting the basic facts and making wild accusations about me. I tried to steer things back to the truth when my turn came but the *gendarme* was wavering, toying with the coins of EXHIBIT 'C' and casting about for a solution that would please both parties. He asked me if I was still hungry. When I said 'Yes!' he grasped at this, asking me if I'd like to take the chicken with me in the car, to which I firmly replied 'No!' I've no idea what direction he would have taken next for the whole drift of things then took a dramatic turn.

Right in the middle of another excited outburst from the *patron*, a totally new element entered the fray as two people emerged from the dining-room and, to my delighted surprise, started shouting at the *patron*. I never did know the nature of their own discontent nor did I really care. The important thing right then was that they had entered the lists in my defence, blasting the surprised *patron* with a rapid flow of French. I did not understand much of this but one statement was clear: 'This is no way to behave to a foreigner who will get a very poor impression of our country!' The man who said this then threw a fifty-franc note in the general direction of the *patron* who promptly threw it back. It floated lazily down in front of my face and I grabbed it, handing it back to its rightful owner. The ruckus then began to subside. The *patron* knew he was defeated, the *gendarme* was off the horns of his dilemma, my new allies had salvaged the honour of their country and I had emerged a victor of sorts. All that remained was to recover my raincoat. When the *gendarme* asked the *patron*: '*Où est l'imper' de monsieur?*' he sheepishly took it off a hook and gave it to me, obviously having thought better of leaving it on the floor behind the bar. I thanked the *gendarme* and my new friends, then left the bar and the town, still feeling hungry but not caring any more. On the outskirts of the town we passed a sign displaying its name: Castillon la Bataille! Seemed appropriate.

Up the Rhône to Lyon

In late April we left Agde, arriving at Aigues Mortes in the evening after a long, tiring day to share our mooring there with a placid Camargue horse tethered on the bank. He was a pleasant companion during our brief stay, becoming a large but friendly fixture at the end of the ramp. Joss, on the other hand, had quite a different view of things, clearly intending to give him a very wide berth in spite of the Dalmatian's reputed traditional fellowship with horses. They did, after all, sleep at one time in the stables and run happily with carriages almost under the horses' hooves but Joss had never heard anything about all that. To her, horses were nothing more nor less than ridiculously oversized dogs and probably dangerous to boot. Joss, however, still had to go down the ramp once in a while for a walk, bringing her terribly close to the 'big dog'. This must have slipped her mind when, next morning, she sauntered down the ramp, sleepy and a little slow to absorb some of the more salient features of the immediate landscape. When she finally looked up her entire field of vision was filled by just one enormous white 'dog' and panic seized her. Retreat was her only thought, very rapid retreat. Although Joss has many fine qualities, courage in the face of the enemy is not one of them. She took instant evasive action, with a leap and sudden reversal of direction that astonished Melodie, followed by a wild scratching scramble up the ramp to regain the security of the only safe place she knew in a confused, constantly shifting world. No persuading could get her out again while that 'thing' was still around.

A day or so later we stopped briefly at Gallician, our jumping-off place for the Rhône. From there I phoned the nearby lock to get the latest word on the Rhône current, reported by the lock-keeper to be *moyen* or average, and Melodie, taking advantage of the sun and canalside water, did a massive wash, later to hang dripping from ropes stretched from bow to stern. Very early the next morning we went through the St Gilles lock into the Petit Rhône, shortly reaching its junction with the Rhône proper. At this point the Rhône's width is constricted, markedly increasing the speed of the current. Several people have told me that, even with their boats at maximum speed, they have remained for many anxious minutes in this part of the river, hardly moving past the trees on the bank. They just had to hang on, creeping forward by inches, until the current slackened as the river widened upstream. We had no such trouble, but *Lionel* even at maximum cruising speed was moving no faster in the swift current than the very slow speed permitted in the canals. It is certainly clear that anyone wishing to cruise these waters should have a boat with sufficient speed to master a current that, at times, can reach eight knots. The only alternative is to get a tow from a barge, as is sometimes done.

Avignon provided the first reasonable night's mooring, although we were forced to tie up at the end of the commercial quay, reserved for working barges. There we spent the night, praying that priority customers would not disturb our sleep and left at dawn the following morning under a clear blue sky, slipping downstream through mirror-calm water past the Pont St Bénézet brilliantly lit by the rising sun. This, of course, is the famous Pont d'Avignon which everyone knows about from the song. Now truncated in mid-stream, the narrow bridge once carried pedestrians across the river but, according to the guidebook, was never wide enough to make possible the dance described in the song. However, both the legend and the song will thankfully survive such dashes of scholarly cold water.

Once on the river again, *Lionel*'s new VHF radio telephone, installed in Béziers, started to pay dividends. With it I could now inform lock-keepers who, what and where we were so that, barring other traffic, the locks could be prepared for our arrival. With information available about boats approaching from both directions life was easier for everyone. Our problem with the radio was never fully understanding the lock-keepers' replies, because of accent and radio distortion but mainly an inability to extract precise meaning from a rapid flow of French. It didn't seem to matter a lot, however, since the main thing was to inform the lock-keeper. I usually seemed to accomplish this in spite of what, to him, must have been my own peculiar accent.

During the afternoon, the Mistral began to blow strong and cold down the river, soon kicking up waves that might concern the smaller boats and it wasn't long before we came across two tubby little steel boats, lashed together side by side as they gamely fought their way upstream. We shared the next lock with them, watching with interest what happened when they emerged from it into the unprotected upstream water where the waves were even higher. Using all the limited power at their disposal, they barely managed to struggle from the lock, weaving wildly from side to side and bouncing like flotsam on the waves. In the ensuing wild ride, the ropes holding them together snapped and the boats separated, one to seek refuge against the shore and the other stoutly pushing on at a speed that scarcely made the effort seem worth while. When last seen far to our stern, the little boat was just a white speck bobbing and lunging in its own cloud of spray.

We ran for ten hours that day against wind and current. At the end of it we were tired and looking forward to the quiet mooring at Viviers, one of the nicest on the Rhône, a river with few enough good ones. As we came around the last bend, however, the long stone quay was completely obscured by an enormous tour boat taking up the entire length of the wall with a barge tucked in behind it. The boat was the *Fleur du Rhône*, a vast floating hotel, capable of carrying over two hundred passengers on cruises of a week or more. By river standards this was a big boat, over a hundred yards long with other dimensions to match. We were dismayed to see this green and white monster dominating the quiet little village quay and leaving us nowhere to moor. After a very long day, any thought of searching for another mooring was out of the question so I brought *Lionel* in to moor alongside the *Fleur du Rhône*. The wind was so strong that, at the last moment, it slapped the boat savagely against the massive steel flank of the leviathan with a crunch that sounded bad but damaged little. Once secured I went aboard the big boat and obtained the captain's permission to stay the night. This granted, I returned to find an English yacht, in a similar fix, moored outside *Lionel*.

The *Fleur du Rhône* may well have been this captain's last important command. Two weeks later, with the Rhône in full flood, it was going downstream, fortunately without passengers, when it tried to go under a bridge at La Voulte. At the last moment, when it appeared the boat wouldn't make it through because of high water, the order was supposedly given to go hard astern. It is hard to know what effect that had on the inevitable final result but the boat hit the bridge and became stuck there. The crew scrambled up ladders on to the road above but the *Fleur du Rhône* could not be saved, even the awesome power of a large pusher failing to budge it. The strong current then went to work, sinking the boat across the navigable channel and blocking traffic for several days. By this time the *Fleur du Rhône* was beyond saving. It could only be cut up under water with torches and removed piece by piece in three-hundred-ton chunks. This accident, one of the worst in recent years, confirms the Rhône's reputation as a hazardous river but the surprising thing is that the captain had twenty-five years' experience on big rivers like the Neckar, the Mosel and the Rhine, all amply provided with hazards but perhaps not low bridges. The French claim, possibly with cause, that the Rhône is not like other rivers and requires special knowledge. As one *marinier* commented after the accident: 'Perhaps the Dutchman will take a pilot next time.'

Progress up the Rhône the next day was smooth, thanks largely to the new radio heralding our approach while still several miles from the locks. But coming out of one lock the way ahead appeared blocked by dredgers and a fat pipe stretching across our path. It was not clear how, or even if, one could get through the mess. I advanced slowly and appealed to the lock-keeper by radio for directions. I didn't understand his garbled answer and, repeating the question, only succeeded in eliciting irritated shouts from high overhead. In the meantime, Melodie was waving her arms at the dredger in a 'What are we supposed to do?' kind of way. At last the exasperated lock-keeper and the men on the dredger indicated that the exit was hidden around the corner to the right. And so it was, at the end of the large floating pipe which was regurgitating a steady stream of semi-liquid river bottom.

The overnight mooring we chose at Tournon was a rocky place across the river from its twin town, Tain-l'Hermitage, where vines cover the steep hills, crowned at their top by large white signs announcing the growers' names. The hills are so steep they can only be worked by back-breaking manual effort but produce the famous Hermitage wines, some of which we enjoyed that night in a restaurant with two Danish friends. They left in their boat the following morning but we stayed on for one of the 'free days' that Melodie insists on from time to time, relaxing, reading and watching the river traffic. Surprisingly, there wasn't much; the odd yacht making speedy passage to the south and a few barges. Some of these were the usual blunt-nosed 350-tonners and a few pushers but most were the barges I have always associated with this river: fast, long and thin with pointed bows, the typical Rhône barge. Their lines give them an unexpected elegance compared to canal barges but they have a countervailing scruffiness that makes them look shabby alongside their often immaculately maintained smaller brothers. One also sees, though rarely, the large new hybrid craft designed both for the sea and inland waters but as yet denied access to the industrial heartland of the Rhine by the old Canal Rhône au Rhin not yet brought up to the 'European standard' designed to accommodate such large boats.

The mooring at Tournon was far from ideal. Rocks glared just below the surface at the stern so *Lionel* had to be held away from them with a small anchor, an old one of the 'fisherman' type, the traditional anchor shape, familiar from its common use as a symbol. Our dawn departure was enlivened and delayed by a tiresome struggle to disengage this anchor from the bottom. There being no winch at the stern, the only feeble resources available for the job were my own two arms. But however I pulled, the anchor would not loosen its grip and, finally, in angry frustration, I cut the rope, committing the anchor for all time to the river it seemed so reluctant to be parted from. I did not grieve much at its passing. It was an awkward thing at best, difficult to stow, ineffective in sand or gravel and cussed on a rocky bottom. So good riddance to it. The only other anchor wrestle in my life up to then had been a memorable one on a lake, part of the Rideau Canal in Ontario. The anchor had dragged in a wind but oddly had refused to surface. It was, however, only a small anchor and after a struggle, Melodie and I managed to raise it far enough to see dimly through six feet of water. With horror we saw that the anchor was hooked around an underwater power cable, luckily undamaged. With extreme care we released the cable with a boathook and, much relieved not to be electrocuted, brought the anchor aboard.

Arriving in Lyon during the late afternoon we tied up at the long stone quay on the Saône just upstream of the Perrache bridges. As a sort of footnote to this journey up the Rhône we were surprised to realise that it had taken the same number of days as the downstream trip and that we had stopped in all the same places. There was, however, a substantial difference in the hours run each day and in the fuel consumption. On the southward journey the short December days only permitted six or seven hours' daily running time but in the spring this was extended to an average of ten hours per day. There was a corresponding difference in the fuel burned, the southerly trip requiring about forty-five gallons or about one and a half an hour whereas we needed for the northward journey, an average of nearly two gallons per hour, which, I suppose, is not excessive for such a boat bucking wind and current at close to maximum cruising speed.

Flood

We did not intend to stay in Lyon for more than a few days, having started quite late from the south, but when we were on the point of leaving Melodie came down with a mysterious malaise requiring the attention of a doctor. Judging it prudent, in the case of illness, not to attempt communications in an unfamiliar tongue, I went in search of an English-speaking doctor. With the rather doubtful assistance of British Airways such a person was finally found, an appointment made and Melodie delivered to his door. On her return to the boat she reported a surprising diagnosis: vitamin C deficiency, the ailment afflicting seamen on long voyages in early days. In other words, SCURVY! She didn't have the symptoms one reads about, painful joints and teeth falling out, and she certainly ate enough green things but there it was, in 1985 on *Lionel*! I couldn't believe it, nor could Melodie and I am convinced the doctor erred. But she did what she was told and soon improved, with the help of or in spite of, the prescribed diet and medication.

By the time Melodie was well enough to travel we were, alas, trapped in Lyon by the elements. The rains came, water pouring from the sky day after day and combined with the spring run-off from the mountain snows to create flood conditions in the Saône. It was soon more than three feet above normal level, sending down swirling brown water and débris past the line of boats along the quay. Attempting to travel on such a river seemed unwise so we settled down for the flood to abate. Barges continued for a while but going upstream was a slow, costly slugging match against the river with throttles wide open and little forward speed. The water continued to rise but before the flood peaked, making the current far too strong, a few yachts battled their way upstream to Lyon, some taking five hours to cover the last twelve miles. When the flood reached its peak, four feet above normal, every space along the generous quay was occupied by barges or yachts, newcomers being forced to moor outside the boats already there. In one short section of the quay there were two Danish boats, one English, two Canadian, a large Norwegian cruiser, its young owner just off a Persian Gulf oil-rig, and briefly, a small Dutch boat, a German yacht and a French motor yacht damaged in the flood upstream where the locks were closed and passage permitted over the open weirs.

The quay at Lyon was a narrow cobbled roadway separated from the street ten feet above by a high stone wall. Not a great deal happened on it except for the parking of cars but two or three times a week a group of well-dressed men would gather there with oddly-shaped instrument cases. These contained hunting horns, the coiled brass affairs with wide trumpet mouths the French used to carry, and may still do, when riding to hounds. The men, from business or the professions, came to the quay to practise the piercing, not always harmonious, music produced by these instruments, apparently in the belief that, on the quay, the citizens of Lyon would be less rudely disturbed. Those of us in boats nearby had no such preferred treatment, being exposed to the full blast of six or seven unco-ordinated horns. When the practice got under way, the men would stand facing the stone wall, looking as if engaged in group bladder-relief, with the horn mouths facing

backwards over their shoulders, pointing, not at the expensive apartments across the street but directly at us. And there they would remain, practising *ad nauseam* the same fanfare over and over again. The music was repetitive, often discordant and always loud. When the gentlemen were in full musical flight, the sound coming from them overpowered all else, even the considerable noise of traffic from the street. I was consequently alarmed one day when they set up to play opposite *Lionel* and I approached the leader with a polite request to move a few yards along the quay. Being an understanding man, he graciously consented. What I didn't know then was that a few days later we would be having lunch with him, his family and two Canadian friends in a large old apartment high above our mooring and there to hear a marvellous record of the same hunting horns as they really should be played.

It was also on this quay that I observed from the wheelhouse a brief little incident, charming in its way and one of those facets of life that make the French the people they are. Glancing idly in the direction of the quay one afternoon, I saw a car come down the ramp from the street and stop. An attractive girl in her twenties jumped out wearing bright-red slacks, went quickly between two parked cars, pulled down the slacks, squatted on the cobbles and did what, quite clearly, she most desperately had to do. Many women would almost die of shame to be seen doing this in a public place but not this girl. While still squatting, she looked up, saw me sitting in the boat ten yards away and smiled sweetly. I smiled back. She then stood up, assembled her clothes, hopped into the car and was gone. Her act of bravado symbolised the frank acceptance by the French of life's unavoidable basic facts that I find refreshing. A spade after all is a spade. This girl was also, I suspect, paying the penalty for living in what is still largely a male-dominated society that has for generations provided convenient, albeit unpleasant, *pissoirs* for the male population, even in the small villages, but has only recently begun to equip its urban centres with lavatories for women as well.

For several weeks *Lionel* had been blessedly free of the mechanical or electrical crises that seem to dog the lives of boat captains. It had been an unusually long time and it was only reasonable that something should happen soon. And it did, once again through the agency of the captain himself, *Lionel*'s onboard, amateur mechanic. While in Lyon, a major centre for barges and their special needs, I had been able to re-stock the boat's supplies of the various filters required for the engine and its fuel system. When I examined these new filters a nagging doubt invaded my head about whether I had earlier installed the correct oil filter. Since the only way to be sure was to have a look, I removed the filter, found it to be the right one after all and put everything back together again. Up in the wheelhouse I started the engine, letting it run for a few minutes. I don't know why I did this nor why, much later, I looked in the engine-room. But I did and found a horrible mess. Black engine oil was everywhere, apparently disgorged under high pressure from the oil filter in a spray which had spread the stuff over everything and it now lay in dark puddles on the floor. As I might have known, the filter casing had been improperly installed, leaving a gap through which the oil had squirted. It was the kind of thing I seemed to be developing an unsuspected talent for and I didn't like it much. After a pause for self-abasement, cleaning up the mess and re-installing the filter casing I asked Melodie overhead to start the engine so I could check for leaks. Showing an unusual sensitivity to the engine's vital signs, she promptly turned it off on seeing the oil pressure at zero. The sump was, indeed, quite empty, its entire contents having been thrown up in what was surely one of the messiest and fastest oil changes in the long history of the internal combustion engine!

The flood started to subside at last, bringing more activity on the river but few boats could master the current still flowing strongly at nine miles an hour and, at the bridges, undoubtedly faster. Even the powerful long Rhône tankers struggling slowly upstream had to concede defeat at the bridge above our mooring. The river was narrow at this point, too narrow for the long boats to turn, so the only alternative was to back downstream. Never a simple manoeuvre, it was complicated in their case by having to go backwards through two other bridges and around a corner before the river was wide enough for them to turn. Although less difficult than it might appear because, in the fast current, the boats could maintain steerage way even while going backwards, it still could not have been easy putting a large boat stern first through the relatively narrow arch of a bridge and I am glad I wasn't the one who had to do it.

Watching boats trying to pass the upstream bridge became a spectator sport during the last few days of the flood. It was a particularly tricky place because the river was shallower and the current faster due to the presence on the bottom of fifty thousand tons of stone, placed there to prevent river erosion above a new subway excavation. One day a Danish friend, in a hurry to get home, attempted to get past this bridge in a boat with a maximum speed of ten miles per hour. He managed to get through the wild turbulence below the bridge but remained under the arch, motionless with throttle wide open. There he stayed for several minutes before giving up, backing slowly through the bridge before spinning around in the current and returning to the quay. An unloaded 350-ton barge, unwisely attempting the same thing, was carried violently by the current into a pier. The collision demolished its wheelhouse and the barge remained wedged under the arch for several hours with the forlorn, life-jacketed *marinier* waiting in the bow for a powerful tug to pull his boat free.

By the third week in May the river had almost returned to its normal level. It was safe to leave Lyon and after three weeks we were certainly ready to go. Holland, our destination, was still a long way off.

Dogs

Dogs and boats generally seem to go pretty well together. Although a boat could hardly be a dog's idea of the perfect terrain, dogs are adaptable beasts, taking life much as it comes. Most of them are, in any case, so imprinted on their human companions that they will put up with a great deal just to be with them. This was certainly true of Joss, whose attachment to us both was glue-like, following one of us around everywhere a few steps behind. This was fine but on a boat where there is much coming and going in a small space, at times, a little awkward. And we often found ourselves stumbling over this loyal follower as we rushed to do something urgent. For that reason Joss was a temporary prisoner in the wheelhouse during the more hectic moments aboard. This same fondness for our company made her complain bitterly to the world at large when left alone on the boat, something she detested. Long, pathetic, ululating cries emerged from the wheelhouse that touched the hearts of passers-by and must have driven to distraction those unlucky enough to be on nearby boats during these pitiable spells of loneliness.

147

In France, it is a rare barge that doesn't have a dog on board, often a *berger* or German shepherd and many smaller boats also carry dogs. Bringing them into France which, unlike Britain, has no quarantine period, only requires certificates of good health and rabies inoculation but in my experience not even these are often looked at. Transportation by air certainly has its own special requirements to do with cages, tranquillisers and airport regulations and flying cannot be very pleasant for a dog but it doesn't last long. Joss is always sedated before crossing the Atlantic but once we slightly overdid this and she arrived in Paris drugged to the gills, staggering around for an hour afterwards on some dreamy trip of her own, eyeballs half-rolled back in her head. But whatever the problems, they are minor and greatly outweighed by the advantages of having a dog on one's boat. For people who like dogs the companionship and amusement they provide are obvious but there is a more practical side. When travelling in a strange country on a boat that must, inevitably, be left unoccupied at times, a dog is a good protection against casual theft and vandalism. I have, often enough, seen the look on visitors' faces when faced with Joss at the wheelhouse door. Startlingly marked, standing on hind legs and barking, I know she is a severe deterrent. And I know also that I would not attempt to board a barge with a German shepherd or even some smaller dog prowling its decks when the owner was absent.

The barge dogs are a bit like their owners, self-contained, independent and disinclined to strike up casual conversations with strangers. But the dogs that almost every lock seems to boast are not at all like this. There are, of course, the unapproachable chained ones, considered to be *méchant*, their chains making matters even worse as their boring days wear on. And sometimes there are the dogs used for *la chasse*, amiable, garrulous types, usually segregated from the common herd in their own caged runs. But it is the lucky free rovers that the canal user is most likely to meet, a motley collection of most impure ancestry, sprinkled lightly over the locks of France. Most have one or two of these curious, ever-famished scroungers who dash out to meet every new arrival, wandering up and down in hopes of a little food, their noses hanging over the edge of the lock as the boat rises or falls in the lock chamber. For a brief moment one may find one's face and their whiskered, questing snouts a few inches away as one passes them in an unexpectedly intimate and amusing face-to-face confrontation.

The lock dogs are a pleasant diversion as one passes through but a boat dog is with one all the time and brings aboard with it a few problems it is well to face. Dogs can and do fall in the water. Our own dog has done this several times, fortunately always at a quay where it has not been difficult to fish her out. Although caused normally by over-casual footwork, any number of things may be the cause of accidents.

On one occasion Joss, with leash attached, made a great leap for the shore only to have the leash catch on the boat's railing, stopping her cold in mid-flight. She plummeted like a stone into the water from which she was dragged, legs thrashing. At the time she was wearing a chain training collar, a poor thing for pulling a dog out of the water and she has since been equipped with a sturdy woven leather one, a ready handle in emergencies less likely to throttle her during subsequent rescues.

Our 'dog overboard' incidents have been mild compared to those one hears about from others. A friend, delivering a big barge to Paris for a client, with his wife and their black Labrador aboard, was forced to wait several minutes on the Seine at a bridge under construction. He cruised back and forth waiting for the lights to change and finally saw people on the shore wildly waving their arms to attract his attention. He at last realised that his dog was in the water, patiently swimming back and forth with the boat but by then was all done in and nearly finished. Our friend luckily was able to save him by going down the high side of the barge on a ladder and pulling the exhausted dog on to the deck. In another incident, a dog fell off a hotel barge into a lock, not a good place to be because of the turbulence and the danger of being squashed between boat and lock wall. In this case there was little water left for the dog after the big boat had filled the lock but it found a small spot to swim in and when a life-belt was lowered from the boat it had sense enough to put the front part of its body through the ring and, holding on with its forelegs, was lifted safely to the deck. Not all dogs, however, have such remarkable sangfroid and not all the endings are happy ones. With a dog aboard one must be constantly on the watch.

Long days aboard a boat create the other major problem. For this reason we have always tried to avoid long trips with no 'dog stops' but it's not always possible, especially on rivers where moorings of any kind are sometimes hard to find. Then there are only two options open to the dog: bear the internal pressures with patient fortitude or throw all training to the winds and 'do it' on the deck. Only once or twice in several years of cruising has Joss been driven unwillingly to the second alternative. Normally she simply hangs on. Locks, even the big ones on the Rhône are sometimes places for a quick run but locks are often busy places with quays that may be hard to reach and lock-keepers reluctant, at times, to give permission. We only managed it once on the Rhône, the lock-keeper having given his O.K. over the radio with the admonition to be quick because a 'barge is coming in ten minutes'. We immediately leapt into action, putting out the ramp and hurrying Joss up it on to the lockside where we hoped she would find a sympathetic patch of grass. She trotted ashore and began sniffing around casually as the minutes ticked by. Standing at the railing of the boat we fretted and willed her, for God's sake, to get on with it. But there's no hurrying these things. In her own good time, the perfect spot was found, the mission accomplished and calmly she wandered back down the ramp as the barge approached.

La Seille

We left Lyon on a bright sunny morning, heading upstream on the now docile Saône to continue our journey to Holland. But there was time to put in since the Canal de l'Est, part of the route north from the Saône over the watershed to the Moselle, was closed for repairs until the second week in June. This gave us a leisurely two or three weeks to explore the little river Seille and the upper reaches of the Saône. It could not have been a better time and a better place to while away the days in agreeable indolence. The sun shone, the air was warm, the wind was still and both these rivers offered the peaceful waters and gentle scenery needed for this kind of thing.

We stopped overnight at Mâcon, once again close by the malodorous riverside *pissoir* we don't seem able to avoid, and reached the Seille the following day. It is a quiet little stream in normal times, running from the Saône about eighteen miles upstream to the head of navigation at Louhans in the heart of the Bresse region, renowned for its poultry. Not much happens on the Seille and that is its special charm. It runs through a closed-in, rolling countryside with few villages and little else along its banks but fields, trees and cows. It carries hardly any traffic, has only four tired old locks and is wonderfully free of the disturbance from road or rail that often shatters the peace in other places. The Seille is a place apart, isolated from the noisy world around it, almost forgotten and little known.

Even the entrance to the river is almost concealed from the Saône and the approach to it is curving, shallow and tricky with sand banks pushing out from the shore on both sides. Taking it very slowly and expecting to go aground at any moment we gained the first lock without incident and found ample water beyond.

The Seille had only just returned to its normal level after the recent flood which had turned the quiet stream into a roaring torrent. The lock-keepers could talk of nothing else and the evidence was everywhere, sand in the lock machinery, débris of all kinds thrown up on the bank brush, weeds, and bits of plastic caught on branches high above the water. It was hard to believe that this gentle little river could have been so boisterous. Certainly, during a few enchanted days in May, the Seille offered Melodie and me its most composed and serene aspect as we slid quietly along past overhanging trees and newly green pastures sprinkled with the white blobs of Charollais cattle.

We moored for the first night by a tall stand of trees with a meadow climbing gently towards woods hiding all but the spire of a village church and the much turreted roof of a château. The curious cows formed a staring reception committee as we tied up but soon, becoming bored, wandered off to complete their daily ration of fresh spring grass. It was an idyllic setting in which even the barbecue struck a foreign note, but, like the cows, we had to eat. Over chicken and wine we soaked up the bucolic peace of the lovely place as the setting sun slowly drained colour from the fields and trees. There was not a sound but the birds settling for the night, the mooing of a cow in a distant meadow and little fish jumping in the river as it slipped quietly by.

In another shining day we followed the river upstream through three more locks, for the first time encountering the idiosyncrasies that make them a little different. They were not provided with places to disembark at either end nor with ladders on the gates nor, in all cases, with lock-keepers and the banks at the locks were usually overgrown with bushes. The only possible access to the lock was by climbing the gate and this Melodie had to do from the bow of the boat. All the lock equipment was old, difficult to operate and the gates were badly clogged with sand making them reluctant to open fully. Even the mechanism for working them had its irritating foibles but how can one complain about small things like that on such a lovely river?

As the meandering Seille led us sedately upstream we constantly expected a road or railway track to appear around the next corner and shatter the extraordinary spell cast by this river. But none ever did. It was almost like being travellers in some minuscule time-warp, the modern world with all its noise and pointless bustle left somewhere else altogether. In the whole length of the river there were no more than two small villages, hardly another sign of life except for the motionless figure of an occasional fisherman enjoying his afternoon off and birds. Birds were everywhere: mute swans raising new families, cygnets sometimes riding on their parents' backs, mallards, teal, black and white tufted ducks, grey herons, moorhen skittering across our paths, blackbirds, crows, magpies, collared doves, cuckoos (heard but never seen), blackcaps, goldfinches, common sandpipers and great crested grebes hull down in the water, their upright necks and knobbly heads looking like floating sticks.

Close to the head of navigation we were thwarted in an attempt to enter Louhans by a pollution barrage across the river. But it didn't matter much for we had little need of a town. The days continued warm and bright so we retraced our steps to wander a few more days in the Seille's green solitude. We moored to the grassy banks, were regularly inspected by the cows, we ate, slept, read, lay in the sun and, greatest pleasure of all, swam naked in the cool brown water. It was hard to tear ourselves away but our goal was still far to the north and we were forced to join the real world once again. With much reluctance we left the enchanted Seille, went through the last lock and returned to the Saône.

The upper Saône

After leaving the Seille, we intended to moor first at Tournus, where the quay had been flooded on our way south. This was the case again, the Saône still not having completely returned to pre-flood levels so we were forced to seek a mooring further upstream at Chalon. It is because of this kind of thing that it is prudent, on large rivers, to moor long before it begins to get dark. River moorings are often hard to find with long distances between them and a search late in the day can mean stumbling around in the dark, which, on a river, is certainly a game for fools. If one starts early, there is at least a chance of finding another mooring in daylight if the first one proves to be no good.

At Chalon, where we'd had so much trouble mooring on our southward journey there now seemed a better alternative, at the end of the marine pontoon near our Canadian friends who had arrived earlier from Lyon. But it was a trickier place than it first appeared, being swept by a surprisingly strong lateral river current. It all looked innocent enough until I made our final approach to the lock when *Lionel* was inexorably carried sideways towards our friends' yacht. I was helpless, able to do nothing but stop all forward motion, as our heavy boat was pushed broadside by the current against their immaculate white plastic craft. Fortunately both boats were well protected with bumpers and there was only a soft, squishing thump as they met, causing no damage, although it is hard for me to believe that the yacht is not now half an inch or so narrower than its makers intended.

After a day in Chalon we moved on to St Jean de Losne from where the car was retrieved from Lyon by Melodie and taken to Auxerre by me. Having done that we'd had enough of cars and trains for a while and travelled up river to moor on the pleasant stepped quay at Auxonne, a nice little river town whose main feature is the fortification and barracks where Napoléon served briefly as a young officer of eighteen. It now contains a small museum where much is made of

154

Napoleon's rather slender connection with the town. We duly visited the museum but it was events on the river that captured our attention.

It was the time of Auxonne's annual *fête nautique*, a kind of mixed media regatta involving as many people doing as many different things as possible during the short afternoon. I never tire of these occasions with their bubbling enthusiasm, their earnest strivings, their successes, their failures and the surprises that unfold. At Auxonne on that sunny afternoon there were all the usual things going on: little motor-boats dashing here and there, half-hearted sailing races, becalmed wind surfers and water-skiers by the score, but as the afternoon wore on, greater challenges were thrown at the skiers and success more rarely achieved. Total failure met every attempt to construct wobbly human pyramids, doomed from the start to end in watery confusion and, much to everyone's relief, they were finally abandoned. The grand finale got under way as a boat came at speed through the bridge towing six girls in line abreast, each holding a large French flag. The trouble began when the whole ensemble tried to turn in the river before making their majestic way back past the spectators on the bank. As they started to do this, one girl fell. Then the rot set in. One after the other went down flags and all, leaving only the boat with its rope trailing sadly behind. Feeble efforts were made by all to regroup but it was too late by then to recover from the fiasco and, although that was the end of the grand finale, there was to be one of another sort.

Watching the *fête nautique* was a small crowd of spectators sitting on the grass beside the river, dressed in their brightest summer clothes; a gay and carefree lot, enjoying the sun and each other. Then we noticed, at the end of the afternoon and certainly before the spectators did, a determined herd of brown cows plodding homeward down the river bank, on a collision course with the crowd watching the *fête nautique*. We were glued to our binoculars, momentarily transfixed, and hardly believing what was about to happen. The cows, not to be deterred by anything and certainly not a *fête nautique*, just lumbered on across the grass, scattering surprised spectators right and left in a confused mêlée, certainly more amusing for us across the river than for the unfortunates right at its epicentre.

As we cruised upstream the next day through a densely forested stretch, dark trees slipping by on each side, the silence was almost palpable until we began to sense something else hard to identify, a periodic muffled 'whump' not only heard but also felt, as if the boat had struck a large soft thing in the water. We had become used to

whatever it was until, further on, there was a very loud bang close to the boat. I knew what that was and the chart confirmed it. Hidden just behind the trees was a *terrain militaire* where the army, Melodie's 'killing machine', was playing with explosives. Joss, badly freaked by bangs of all kinds, retreated swiftly below to seek what refuge there was in her own soft bed, the wombiest and safest place she knew. The wild animals had no such secluded retreat but perhaps had become inured to the noises of the 'killing machine' for not much later, when the bangs had died down, we saw what looked like a small animal swimming across the river, but turned out to be the head of a young deer. Reaching the other side, it climbed up the steep bank, its dark brown back shining wet in the sun, struggled through the brush and vanished quickly in the forest.

After a night in Gray at a ghastly mooring among bulrushes standing in foetid water fed largely by a drain from the dilapidated houses nearby, we hurried away upstream to seek a secluded place in the sweet-smelling countryside far from towns and their odorous effluents. The Saône was now becoming narrower in its upper reaches, twisting its way peacefully past farmland and, in some ways, resembling its little sister Seille, though never quite matching the latter's atmosphere of intimate isolation. But good moorings were strangely hard to find because of heavy growth along the banks and only after much searching did the right one come along at last. It was ideal in its way: secluded, remote from cars, trains or people, screened by trees and perfumed by new-mown hay. We prepared to moor.

Tying a boat, even a large one, to some trees on a bank should be, and usually is, a simple matter. God knows, we've done it often enough and by that time could claim a modest competence in boating skills. But, as everyone with a boat should know, things have a nasty habit of falling apart when least expected. This was such a time. A fresh offshore breeze was blowing as Melodie disembarked with a rope which she tied to a tree. Because the wind was blowing the stern away from the shore I threw her another rope. I asked her to tie it quickly but she said the rope was not long enough. As I manoeuvred the boat to give her more, the first rope came away from the tree and snaked across the grass into the water. I now knew the whole scenario, blow by horrid blow. I had been here before as if in some awful boating nightmare. The second rope joined the first in the river, the boat drifted away, both ropes trailing, leaving Melodie like a castaway on the shore. And the captain, speechless as before, gathered up the wet ropes and manoeuvred the boat for another approach. That time we got it right and I made a mental note to give the crew a short refresher course on knots.

After the confusion of our arrival, it turned out to be a lovely spot, deep in the rich green growth of spring with an old farmhouse the only building in sight across the fields. Hardly a boat ruffled the eddying calm of the river flowing past. The sun spread its warmth every day from a cloudless sky. We swam often, diving naked into the cool and, one hoped, tolerably clean water of the Saône with no one to disturb us except for one brief hour when another boat a little way upstream debouched six other naked swimmers. But they were soon gone, leaving us alone in pastoral peace with only the birds for company. Although largely hidden by profuse spring growth, the sound of their singing filled the hours of the day so richly that we played no music, feeling even that to be an intrusion in this idyllic place.

As we meandered up the Saône, mooring each evening in the countryside, the towns became fewer, most of them small with few shops or other resources. Running short of bread, we stopped briefly at Ray sur Saône but found it too small even to support a bakery. There was, however, an old château on the hill above the village so we walked up through the park surrounding it to have a look. It was a huge, rather plain lithic mass in the arid French manner with little to redeem it architecturally. But it had a magnificent site on the hill, overlooking the valley of the Saône and the hazy Vosges mountains far to the east. The place was owned and, in earlier times, defended by the Barons of Ray, one of whom had been on the Fourth Crusade.

Having done a circuit of the château we came finally to the entrance on the west side and were idly wandering about when a bakery truck drove into the courtyard and a well-dressed woman came out of a door to buy some bread. Melodie, who is more of an opportunist than she would care to admit, was not about to let this chance slip by and advanced briskly on the bakery truck deep in the courtyard. She made her purchase, getting strange glances, while doing so, from the lady of the house. Meanwhile Joss and I, sensitive to the nuances of the situation, distanced ourselves as best we could from the brash tourist trespassing boldly in the private courtyard of the great house to buy a *baguette* from under the very nose of, quite possibly, La Baronne de Ray herself.

By this time the navigable Saône was coming to an end. As we approached the top, the river became very narrow and upstream traffic increased, for the Canal de l'Est was due to open shortly. Passing had now become difficult and, with loaded barges, impossible. If unlucky enough to get behind one, there you stayed, barely moving in the wake of the chugging monster just ahead. When this became our fate, crawling along behind the barge on the open river was a tedious business but when we had to navigate a tunnel, conditions became intolerable. A few yards in front, big engine pounding away and hunkered down in the water, the barge was hardly moving. The noise was bad enough in the confined space of the tunnel but the air was so noxious with diesel fumes that I decided to stop until the barge was clear of the tunnel. With the engine turned off the sudden silence in the dark tunnel was a weird experience we shared with a tiny Swedish sailing-boat with whose occupants we carried on an eerie, echoing chat across the gurgling water of the cavern until the lumbering barge broke into daylight at the far end and we could complete our tunnel passage.

Canal de l'Est

At the top of the Saône several boats were waiting for the canal to open after the three week *chômage*: five commercial barges, a German yacht and *Lionel* at the end of the line. On our arrival there had been some doubt about the precise opening day but early the following morning we were woken by the throbbing, throaty roar of big diesels warming up and knew the canal was, once again, ready for business.

The Canal de l'Est is in two parts, the northern branch being the partly canalised River Meuse and the southern branch, which we would travel, joining the Saône at Corre to the Moselle near Nancy. It is a nineteenth-century canal built to the *Freycinet* or *petit gabarit* standard that can accommodate nothing larger than the standard hundred-and-twenty-five-foot barge. The canal, about seventy-three miles long, climbs over a watershed with the help of many locks and, from the Saône to the summit, has a sombre beauty all its own, winding through dense forests in the hills west of the Vosges mountains. There is a strange feeling of isolation as one travels this canal cut through the densely packed trees with its little companion river, the Coney, burbling beside one most of the way. There are some towns but not many and a few short open stretches which give relief from the forest but it is the forest dense and close that gives this lonely canal its special flavour. It's like gliding hour after hour through a brooding wooded glade whose dark, silent beauty conceals some impenetrable mystery. For two people who have travelled many waterways, this sombre, lovely and secluded canal was an unexpected revelation.

The few towns along the south branch of the canal are not of great interest. Some were knocked about in the fighting that swept through this part of France towards the end of the Second World War and subsequent reconstruction has not greatly helped matters, the towns now lacking much of the charm they once may have had. What old buildings remain reflect the mixed cultural influences of the region, once German Alsace lying not far away to the east. But it was spring and the window-boxes of flowers did much to brighten the otherwise drab streets. We didn't stay long in any of these towns although Fontenoy le Château offered more than most, an attractive little place, thinly spread over the wooded valley of the Coney, with its little tributaries running between gardens and several working mills. An enterprising town council had also provided a surprisingly generous quay with services encouraging visitors to stop there.

As we slowly climbed up through the locks we began to meet the traffic which had started from the other end of the canal after the *chômage*. Because the descending barges had priority, we were often forced to wait below locks for them to pass, a normal fact of canal travel. But we hadn't counted on being attacked by a tractor trimming grass along the towpath with a savage cutting device on the end of an articulated arm. As well as cutting grass it had sucked up gravel beside the canal and spat it out in a sudden, fierce bombardment of small stones which rattled against *Lionel*'s steel hull, bounced on the deck and banged against the windows of the wheelhouse. Realising that damage would soon be done and that the tractor driver was quite unaware of what was going on, we both shouted and waved our arms in a frantic effort to attract his attention. The message finally got through and the tractor thankfully retreated, returning the canal once more to its normal tranquil state.

Épinal is the largest town on the south branch of the Canal de l'Est, reached by a short, narrow and very overgrown branch canal. After a day of slogging up through many locks, Melodie was tired and ready for a rest, so we tied up in the port of Epinal for two days. The only possible mooring, smack in the industrial zone of the city, was a dreary place beside the headquarters of a large trucking concern, set in a sea of asphalt, far from the city centre. But, at least, the walk into town was nice enough, along the bank of the Moselle, wide, shallow and full of rapids. But it was not enough to hold a visitor for long and after two days we moved on.

What remains of the canal north of Épinal cannot match the southern part in scenery or atmosphere. Now more open, the canal surrenders what attractions it has more and more to industry as it approaches its junction with the Moselle. So we pressed on through fifteen more locks, arriving tired at what looked like a pleasant mooring in a little basin just before the next lock. But as I approached the bank under some tall trees the lock-keeper made waving signals to dissuade me, thinking, I suppose, the water was too shallow for us. So we did yet another lock, the old lock-keeper promising *un très bon amarrage* a little further on. I don't know what his idea of 'a very good mooring' could have been but, if it was where we finally tied up, it certainly wasn't mine. We have known a lot of moorings in our time and some pretty dreadful ones, but for pure nastiness, this was a record holder of sorts. We were tired, however, reluctant to go on and, resignedly, stayed put. In simple terms, the *bon amarrage* was the underside of the rear end of a service station on a road some fifteen feet above the boat. At the canal level slime-covered concrete columns rose up to support the dirtier departments of the operation overhead from which concrete steps descended into shallow, stagnant puddles beside the boat, sprinkled liberally with discarded rubbish from above. But here we spent the night, trying to ignore the grotty view close outside the window, concentrating instead on the far bank of the canal. At least there was one advantage to this awful place, for I could fill the tanks with diesel fuel in the morning but as a last image of the Canal de l'Est (branche sud) I could have wished for something a great deal better.

The Moselle

When we entered the canalised Moselle from the Canal de l'Est we were involved in a kind of massive gear change. Of course, this was partly due to the transition from an intimate canal to a river, but much more, I think, because we had arrived in *grand gabarit* country. The scale of everything is different. Here the so-called 'European standard' prevails: most of the barges encountered are 1,350 tonners or larger, dwarfing the normal 350-ton barges seen throughout the French canal system. Locks are correspondingly big to deal with both larger barges and heavier traffic. Even the river itself and its scenery are grander in scale. We were, in a sense, entering a different world where, after the canal, everything seemed to have been blown up two or three times life size. Everything, that is, except *Lionel*.

The Moselle is a very beautiful river, perhaps the most beautiful of all the major European rivers. It is generous in size yet narrow enough for the voyager to feel in contact with both its banks. Wandering north in gentle sweeping curves, it passes first through a rolling pastoral landscape of cultivated fields, meadows and woods, then as the Mosel, it enters Germany and becomes far more dramatic, assuming the image for which it has earned its reputation. On both sides the hills increase in size and steepness until the river occupies only a narrow valley floor between steep slopes entirely committed to the grape; row upon row, vineyard after vineyard as far as the eye can see, upstream and downstream, from bottom to top and, no doubt, far beyond. One can almost imagine all that wine running down the hills into the Mosel, itself becoming a monstrous river of white wine, carrying it all north to ocean ports and thirsty mouths around the world.

This vast wine trade has created the little towns that punctuate the shoreline of the river, giving them prosperity and, in many cases, wide renown for the wines produced. With their cosy half-timbered houses and romantic ruins cresting nearby hilltops, these towns complete the picture and explain the traveller's attraction to this marvellous valley.

It is everything one has imagined and almost everything the tourist trade has touted. But a modicum of clear air and sunshine would seem essential for its full enjoyment. And that's the snag. For us, alas, it was not to be. During our entire week on the river, moisture-laden clouds swirled dankly about the hills, releasing rain or mist at frequent intervals to obscure what we could only assume was the magnificent scenery we had come so far to see. Only once in a while did the roiling vapours draw aside long enough to reveal the briefest glimpses of the river's full scenic impact and we had to make do with that.

The Moselle was no exception to the general river condition, presenting the usual range of mooring problems for a boat like *Lionel*. Large barges were catered for with the kind of widely spaced mooring posts found on the Rhône, little boats had their marinas and almost every village had its own small floating steel pontoon anchored in the river. For *Lionel*, the first were too far apart, the second too flimsy or vulnerable and the third, tempting, but reserved for ferries or tour boats who were certain to demand their rights. There was a great scarcity of anything else and we might have been in difficulty but for a wonderful book of river charts for the Mosel and the Rhine, lent for the voyage by a friend. It was a large (and I assume expensive) volume published in Strasbourg, covering the entire navigable length of both rivers, but the most important thing for us was that our friend, having been that way before in his own barge, had carefully marked the few mooring places. I don't know what we would have done without it.

Having started down the Moselle we bypassed Toul, carrying on to Liverdun, the first mooring marked on our friend's chart. He must have been as desperate as we were for the mooring had many drawbacks but, I suppose, neither he nor we could afford to be picky. It was on the inside of a sharp bend in the river, narrow there and running strong past a high concrete wall supporting a minor road with a deserted hotel half-buried behind trees on the far side. It was pouring with rain. Neither the town of Liverdun nor its reputedly good restaurant were anywhere to be seen. After we had finished tying up, the exposed nature of the place became apparent as two loaded barges whipped around the corner only a few yards from *Lionel* charging downstream like trains. This had the predictable effect: the boat lunged violently first one way then the other, stretching each rope in turn like strings on an oversized bass fiddle. Not knowing how much of this the ropes could take, I once again put on rain gear and went out into the wet to rig extra spring lines which I hoped would muffle the violent rope-testing surges of later barge passings.

And then the next problem presented itself. Rain or no rain, Joss must somehow be got ashore for a walk. This did not look, nor was, easy. The wall we were moored against was six feet higher than the deck and topped with a sturdy ornamental steel fence in which there was but one narrow gap through which Joss might possibly be persuaded to squeeze. The problem seemed not far removed from trying to get a smallish camel to walk through the eye of a largish needle, but, at least, we had to try. With Melodie ashore to cajole from the front and me pushing from behind, we persuaded Joss to venture

up the steep ramp. Finally gaining the top of the wall, she was briefly on her own, separated from us both by fence or ramp. For her own obscure reasons she ignored the gap in the fence and set off for a walk along the narrow ledge between the fence and the fast-flowing river below. This didn't seem like a good idea to me, being pointless, foolhardy in the extreme, even dangerous but she wasn't convinced and resisted our efforts to turn her around for another try at the gap. Good sense prevailed, however, and aiming her once more at the gap she reluctantly wriggled through with Melodie pulling from her side and me again pushing from behind. Going back through the fence, in the direction of home was, thankfully, an easier matter now that Joss knew it could be done.

There are several reasons why Liverdun is etched deep in my memory and it was shortly to spring yet another surprise. It rained throughout our stay there, large puddles having collected by late afternoon on the gravelly surface of the road, at our eye level when standing in the wheelhouse. There had been no traffic on the road and we were grateful that, in spite of its other defects, the mooring was, at least, quiet. But as daylight faded, homeward-bound cars appeared suddenly around a corner with headlights glaring. Although we could put up with that, the cars were travelling fast and, as they hit the puddles, splattered a blended mix of water, dirt and gravel at the boat. It wasn't long before one entire side of *Lionel*, windows and all, was decorated with this gritty porridge. All we could do was wait for the mess to dry and clean it off the following day.

After leaving Liverdun we found ourselves behind a slow-moving barge, the *Grâce à Dieu*, sedately occupying the centre of the river. I tried by both radio and horn signals to tell the barge captain I wished to overtake him but, getting no response, pulled out and started to pass. The barge remained where it was, leaving little enough space for us to get by. As I drew abreast the turbulence from the barge made steering difficult and reduced the effective passing speed until I was hardly gaining on it at all. I thought at the time that the barge must have increased its own speed but later realised that this was only another form of an old phenomenon experienced when passing barges on canals. Our speed was being reduced by the flow of water rushing in to fill the void created by the moving barge. Hardly moving relative to one another, the two of us charged abreast down the fairway, blocking passage to anything that might be coming around the corner just ahead. Something had to be done and since the barge captain clearly had no intention of doing anything, I pushed the throttle forward to maximum RPM. Slowly, very slowly we inched forward through the turbulence, finally picking up speed to leave the stubborn *Grâce à Dieu* thankfully behind and end another useful little lesson in fluid mechanics.

Arriving at Metz in the late afternoon, we tied up with other barges in the industrial zone, having failed to find a more attractive mooring. But it was, in some ways, a fortunate choice for it was an interesting experience to be in the midst of a herd of 1,500-ton leviathans as they milled about in the industrial port. In the context of inland waterways these are large boats and being moored close to them, in fact right under their massive bows, made them seem very, very big and *Lionel* very, very small. It even struck me as slightly ridiculous that these massive brutes and our little boat could even be grouped together under the same generic noun. Yet, for all their three-hundred-foot length and vast bulk they are not the ungainly craft they might appear, being easily handled by a crew of two. The wheelhouse of most could be raised or lowered hydraulically, solving the conflicting problems of forward visibility over a high bow and the need to navigate low bridges. Nearly all had button-controlled power steering, thereby avoiding the countless turns of the wheel needed on smaller barges, and the whole range of electronic devices for communication and navigation at night or in conditions of poor visibility. But the greatest help in close manoeuvring such large craft came from the thrusters which allowed the bows to be moved sideways with ease and a surprising degree of subtlety.

Yet even with all the aids these large barges would still be awkward things without the skill of the men who run them. While we were moored in Metz I could observe the barges close at hand, manoeuvring in and out, mooring, departing, all in the confined space of the port, sometimes in high wind and always with many fixed and moving obstacles to avoid, making the job even more difficult. But the huge boats were handled by their crews with a delicacy not always seen with far smaller craft, being turned or docked with only a few feet to spare. While moored in the port, a 1,500-tonner came in to load grain just in front of *Lionel* where I doubted enough space was even available. I watched the manoeuvre with some concern for our own boat, but I shouldn't have worried. The great barge sidled into the space, a crewman in the bow with intercom guiding the captain. He couldn't even see our boat but brought the huge bows almost to within touching distance of our own.

As a city, Metz was a pleasant surprise. Its position in the north-eastern corner of France has so frequently exposed it to the crushing tides of battle I had expected it to be little more than a reconstructed ruin with wounds so grave that few old buildings remained. Yet the city today shows no sign of the violence that has swirled around and through it. Instead it appears remarkably well-preserved, presenting a homogeneity in its urban fabric that isn't often found in the towns of northern France, especially one like this that has taken the full brunt of war so often in the past.

As I wandered down the streets and through the squares the buildings didn't appear to have suffered at all, only mellowed with the passage of time since the days when they were built. They seemed, at first glance, almost to have come from the same period, even the same hand, so harmonious and coherent is the architecture of the town. Metz has been well-served by the architects and builders of the past and even, in places, by those of the present day which is more unusual. For anyone with the time to stroll the streets and riverside walks Metz is a place of many visual pleasures. But, of these, the greatest by far is the superb Cathedral of St Étienne at the city's heart, a marvel of elegant Gothic, radiant and moving, one of that small band of cathedrals which can truly be called great. At the bottom of the hill on which the cathedral stands, the city is further enhanced by little tributaries of the Moselle which penetrate the lower town, by the waterside paths and the river's island parks. I think I could enjoy living in such a place.

The Moselle at last left France, sliding briefly past Luxembourg to become wholly German as the Mosel. We crossed the border on a Sunday, after going through the deep border lock, and moored at the only available place, a pontoon on the Luxembourg side. Checking through their customs was a charming, almost irrelevant affair. I don't think anyone cared very much but we approached the only official in sight, a comic opera figure in a baggy green uniform, its loose leather belt weighed down on one side by an enormous automatic. His few words of English were soon exhausted during passport stamping but he told us in French where to find the German customs and off we went.

Living up to their reputation for efficiency, the Germans normally use fast patrol boats to roar up to new arrivals and transact their customs business on the go. I had been looking forward to this but, perhaps because it was Sunday, all these boats were tied up at the dock. It seemed odd that such rigorous efficiency could take a day off, even on the sabbath, but being fairly law-abiding travellers, we were determined that Germany should know that *Lionel* and its crew were about to enter the Fatherland. So we trudged for about a mile to the customs post on the highway across the river. But we had wasted our time and energy. They weren't the slightest bit interested in us, the boat, our possibly rabid dog or the contraband we might be smuggling across the border. A little disappointed, we walked another mile in a different direction, to the French customs, feeling it important that they, at least, should know we had left France so that our return later might be free of hassle. The *douanes* made up for the indifference of the Germans by completing a complicated form, bound, no doubt, for bureaucratic oblivion but, duty done, we then walked yet another mile or so back to *Lionel* and continued down the Mosel.

At Bernkastel, the mooring marked in our friend's book posed more problems than at first appeared. A strong current, an angled wall and an insufficiency of things to tie to all worked cleverly together to make the job difficult for all hands. It was a fluid, changing state of affairs in which the current threatened to disrupt everything by carrying the bow away from the wall. When this actually began to happen and Melodie had not yet fastened a rope to prevent the impending crisis, the captain, under the stress of the moment, precipitated another by shouting *Tie it up!* at his loyal and loving crew. This was a mistake. The now not-at-all-loyal or loving crew, in a high state of pique, retired to her cabin in tears. My God, I thought: first scurvy, and now *mutiny!* In his hour of need, the captain stood alone and deserted. But a nearby German, silent witness to the whole miserable episode, came to offer help. Once moored, the captain set about restoring the suddenly shaken morale aboard his craft. This done with remarkable ease he set off with the once-again-loyal and loving crew to explore the famous old wine town.

Of all the towns along the Mosel renowned for wine, Bernkastel is probably the widest known, several of its vineyards bearing famous names known throughout the world. One of them, Bernkasteler Doktor, derives its name from the story of a noble traveller long ago who claimed wine from this vineyard cured his illness. It is a famous vineyard but there are others, producing wine that I have known about for most of my life but rarely drunk. The town attracts visitors by the thousands, arriving by bus, car, bicycle and river tour boat. They come partly for its reputation and partly for the picturesqueness of the old town on the east bank with a concentrated German village charm that has been its undoing. It has everything the tourist is looking for: crooked streets with half-timbered houses festooned with window-boxes, the sensational scenery of the river setting, an old castle on a nearby hill, boat trips, bars, restaurants, tourist shops and all kinds of wine to drink and buy. Certainly it has attractions but the overlying pall of tourism has cast a blight on Bernkastel. Neither Melodie nor I are greatly drawn to such places so after one brief sortie into the old town, we retreated to *Lionel* on the other side of the river and departed downstream the next day with fifteen treasured bottles of the precious local wine.

Further down the Mosel, as its junction with the Rhine came nearer, we encountered more commercial traffic, mostly barges of the larger kind. Feeling very small and unimportant in this crowd of giants we carefully observed all the rules governing river traffic and, in a sense, the Mosel was an apprenticeship to prepare us for the hectic experience of the Rhine soon to come. One of these rules, and an important one, concerns 'blue-flagging', a means by which deviations from normal traffic patterns can be safely carried out. Since, on big rivers like the Mosel and Rhine, barges fighting their way upstream against the current naturally seek slacker water near the bank or on the inside of bends, they must often pass oncoming boats on the 'wrong' side or starboard to starboard rather than the normal port to port. To make all this safe and easily understood, such barges signal their intentions by displaying a blue panel (at one time, a blue flag) and, at night, a flashing white light. The oncoming boat acknowledges the signal by doing the same thing so that both boats know what to do. It is a simple system that seems to work well, but for blue-flagging the Mosel was only child's play to what lay ahead on the Rhine.

On the Mosel there are thirty or more locks, all large enough for Eurobarges and, often beside them, a small lock for pleasure boats. The latter was free but, being less than ten feet wide, too narrow for *Lionel*. There was a small charge for the large locks unless they were shared with a barge. The lock-keepers were understandably uncertain which lock to direct us to and whether we intended to wait for a barge or not. I decided to pay the small fee which greatly accelerated progress, but the question of which lock to use had to be sorted out by radio, difficult enough for me in French and an almost insurmountable obstacle in German. Only by dredging up the tiny resources of a few faintly remembered words could I transmit a short string of nouns unlinked by verbs. It was a laughable effort but, strangely, did the job, the lock-keeper at least understanding that we were too wide to go through the smaller lock.

There were occasions, however, when we did share locks with barges and experienced what it's like to be behind a 1,500-tonner as it gets under way to leave the lock. The large screw of these boats throws back such a wash that it is like being in the full current of a flooding river. We, fortunately, knew about this and remained moored until the turbulence had subsided. Even so, the boat tugged at its bollard with such violence that I feared for the rope and I'm sure that, had *Lionel* not been moored, it would have been sluiced sideways to the back of the lock. And this is what happened to a friend in his fifty-foot yacht which was sent spinning in the lock chamber with near-disastrous consequences for its long mast, carried horizontally on the deck and overhanging bow and stern.

Bird life was not a feature of our journey down the Mosel, due perhaps to the weather or the attention that other things demanded. But on the lower reaches near Koblenz, when passing a blue-flagging 1,350-tonner no more than six yards from *Lionel*'s starboard side, I saw out of the corner of my eye a mother mallard and her new brood of seven ducklings caught by accident in the maelstrom between the passing boats. The barge captain saw them too but there was nothing either of us could do. Everyone was much concerned as the little family was tumbled by the turbulence like so many autumn leaves, paddling like mad this way and that to get out of the way. The mother, as frightened as her offspring, would still, I thought, stick to them through thick and thin. How wrong I was. At the peak of the crisis she abandoned her children to their fate, escaping on the wing from the watery hell. So much for mother love, a mother's instinct and all the rest. When the chips are down, for this lady mallard at least, *sauve qui peut* seemed to be the guiding principle. But far astern, the little ducks were finally re-united with their cowardly mum whom they surely must have viewed in a rather different light from that day on.

At Koblenz, at the end of a long day, the old problem of where to moor recurred with unpleasant familiarity. Two of the likeliest places had to be ruled out when, during a cautious approach, the bow grazed gently on to rock. The little pontoons for ferries were enticing but I didn't fancy being told to move by an irate ferry captain after we had settled down for the night. So we looked more closely at the marinas, cheek by jowl along the north-west bank of the river. Going in among the fragile craft was out of the question but the end of a pontoon in an apparently deserted marina became our mooring for the night and here we stayed before tackling the dreaded Rhine the following day.

The Rhine

The Rhine is a mighty river, the mightiest of Western Europe, the most important and the busiest. Flowing out of the Bodensee (Lake Constance), it traverses northern Switzerland to Basel where it becomes navigable, then charges north for over four hundred and thirty miles to the Dutch border, splitting there into the Lek, the Waal and Neder-Rhine which carry its waters another hundred miles or so before they join the North Sea near Rotterdam. It is an international river, touching five countries and a major trade route over the centuries, piercing the greatest concentration of industry in Europe based on the iron ore of Lorraine and the coalfields of the Ruhr. The Rhine flows through forest, farmland, vine-covered hills and the polluting wastelands of heavy industry. Throughout its length there is a great diversity of terrain and vegetation but its much promoted scenery is scarcer than most imagine. The Rhine of the travel poster certainly exists but it happens over a small fraction of the river's total length and as one travels the Rhine in a boat, the dramatic hills and castles are soon passed, leaving what remains of the long river lacking in scenic interest.

Having descended the Rhine some years before from Basel to Holland in a large German tour boat, I had been surprised by the general blandness of the river scenery. But there was nothing bland about some of the Rhine's other features which made a lasting impression on us both; the river's great size, its massive power, its swift, swirling current, its enormous locks and, above all, the incredible traffic it carried. At any one time, fifteen or more boats might be seen coming and going on the river: barges of all sizes from old 350-tonners all the way up the scale to the newest 2,000-ton giants, 5,000-ton pusher-trains and, on the lower Rhine, even small sea-going ships. I recall thinking at the time that this was not a river to be entered lightly in a small boat.

It was because of this earlier trip and the Rhine's fearsome reputation gathered from others that Melodie was apprehensive about our coming voyage on the river. I knew that she faced the prospect with little enthusiasm, always having favoured the calm security of canals over the challenging uncertainty of rivers, and she had only reluctantly agreed to this route north. Melodie knew, however, that the friend who had lent us his book of charts had taken a pilot aboard for his voyage on the Rhine and she campaigned quietly all the way from the south of France for us to do the same. I had no strong objections to this and there were even some indications that it might be obligatory for a boat over fifteen tons, although the only regulations I could get my hands on were in an all but impenetrable German and didn't seem clear on this point. I therefore probed no further although I had, in reserve, the telephone number of a pilot based in Koblenz. But arriving in the city, we found no convenient place to moor and I shied away from the problem of talking to whoever might answer the phone. My few words of German certainly wouldn't stretch to conversation with a perfect stranger, most likely the pilot's wife. So, in the end we did without a pilot and, during two action-packed days on the river, felt no loss because of his absence.

The morning of our departure from the marina at Koblenz dawned bright and sunny but the weather soon degraded into the kind of thing that had dogged us for a week. Throughout the day showers and occasional fierce squalls swept across the countryside reaching a climax in the evening with a rocketing thunderstorm. But weather was the least of our worries as we slipped down the Mosel, through the city of Koblenz and poked our bows tentatively into the Rhine, expecting to see a river full of charging boats. Strangely, as *Lionel* entered the big bend where the two rivers join, there wasn't a boat in sight. But they were there all right. As we turned the corner to go downstream the peaceful impression rapidly vanished. Boats appeared from nowhere, soon crowding one's field of vision in all directions. There were boats in every part of the river, upstream and downstream, coming at us, going away from us, passing us in both directions on both sides. There was even the wreck of a Dutch barge, a grim, half-submerged reminder of the Rhine's dangers.

In a frenzy of blue-flagging we weaved our way through the heavy traffic, frequently altering course to give room to boats coming upstream on our starboard side. To make the whole business a little more exciting, visibility was never good during our passage of the Rhine, the approaching boats being colourless blobs as they emerged from the grey industrial haze. This created problems for Melodie who, even with binoculars, often had trouble seeing, until the last moment, whether an approaching boat was displaying a blue panel or not. She had the binoculars glued to her face for most of those two days, peering down the river and shouting at me so I could alter course when she saw a blue panel. She would then rush to put out our blue flag, made from one third of an old French *tricouleur* and, when the boat had passed, take the flag in again. With so many boats, Melodie's time was completely taken up gazing forward into the haze, warning me, putting out the blue flag and taking it in each time with hardly a moment left even to go below for a pee.

Going down the Rhine was like being on a giant assembly-line, the work at hand demanding total concentration with no pauses for anything else. Even eating had to be done on the fly with hastily assembled bits of bread and cheese, eaten by Melodie as she examined the river through her binoculars and by me at the wheel. It was certainly no sightseeing trip. Andernach, Remagen, Godesburg, Bonn, Cologne all slipped by, almost unnoticed in the haze. We were so busy and the weather so bad, the banks of the river became a grey blur of distantly seen trees and buildings. Some stretches were certainly more attractive than others and the town skylines made brief impressions, especially the wonderful twin spires of Cologne's cathedral. And there were some elegant new suspension bridges but the dominant note of the Rhine from Koblenz to Holland was one of commerce and industry, increasing in impact as we neared the Ruhr. Melodie claims that, for her, this voyage will always remain in memory as only a fuzzy view through binoculars of a smog-laden river with boats coming at her bearing vague smudges that she couldn't be sure were blue panels or not.

In that first day on the Rhine, with the help of the river current, we covered eighty-seven miles at an average speed of twelve miles per hour. Arriving at Düsseldorf in the late afternoon, we searched for a mooring, the only one we'd have to make on the Rhine. Cruising slowly down the long quay, we turned and came back, having found nothing suitable. There were any number of the floating pontoons used by tour boats but all warned us off with signs. The industrial port south of the city looked most unpromising as did the odd marinas on the river. The only other possibility and a poor one was on a bend of the river as it enters Düsseldorf. We had noticed it before but, because of its location and the problems it presented had relegated it to an 'if all else fails' category. But all else had failed and it now became the best hope of a very bad lot.

The chosen spot had few attractions. It was on a sharp bend of the narrow, fast-flowing river against large square steel posts, four to six yards apart, standing free of a fifteen-foot-high stone wall with a street above. Steps led down from the street to a landing place at water level. A strong, gusting wind drove rain down the river where large barges hurtled past a few yards away. It combined in one unpleasant package nearly all those things that one tries to avoid in a mooring but there was no choice, we had to make the attempt. Bouncing in the wash from the barges, we approached the mooring, the idea being that Melodie would try to get a bow rope around one of the big posts. As I held the boat in place she tried but failed to do this. Her arms wouldn't reach around the post and, when she tried swinging the rope around, she was unable to catch the end of it. At the wheel, I was fully occupied just keeping the boat stable in the wind and current and, unable to help her, was desperately searching my brain for another way to get a rope fastened to something solid.

It was at this critical moment, from out of the blue on the street high above our heads, that a man appeared and offered help. It was like a small miracle. Although Melodie could not throw a rope high enough to reach him, I left the wheel for a moment, flung a rope to our Düsseldorf Samaritan and got one around a steel post at the stern. Our kind helper then came down the steps and together we rigged an amazingly complex network of mooring lines and springs to hold *Lionel* securely in that exposed and turbulent place.

The helpful man from the street, it turned out, was an experienced yachtsman with an Atlantic crossing under his belt. He knew all about ropes and knots, showing amazing expertise that was dazzling but needlessly sophisticated. Nevertheless, our gratitude to this man was boundless. A bottle of wine and a few words seemed a poor way to say 'thank you' but that was all we had.

The following morning, untangling the cat's cradle of ropes rigged the evening before took much longer than expected, due mainly to the yachtsman's elegant and intricate knots, efficient no doubt but mean devils to undo, requiring several minutes' work on each with a sharp tool. Holland was still eighty-seven miles away and another long day's cruise lay ahead. Traffic was still heavy on the river, the wash of countless boats mingling randomly to produce waves that rocked the boat eccentrically and made steering harder work than usual. As on the previous day we were both constantly alert for the blue panels of approaching boats and the required course changes. But as the river widened, the boats became dispersed and there was less need for blue-flagging than before. On the Rhine, however, one can never relax and it was finally a considerable relief to reach Lobith, the Dutch border town and tie up in the peace and quiet of the special customs harbour there. Having completed the frenetic two-day trip down the Rhine I felt glad to have done it, but perhaps once was enough. Melodie, I knew, could never be persuaded to go on that particular river again.

Into the Low Countries

It has always amazed me that the countries of Europe, packed for so long cheek by jowl, should still retain such distinct and separate personalities, especially in modern times when mass media of all kinds, increased mobility, outside influences and the Common Market must tend to reduce rather than strengthen national differences. But it is not so, or not yet and one can only be grateful for it. When crossing almost any European frontier one senses the immediate difference, a composite of the people, their language, attitudes, customs, culture, food and the towns they live in. Nowhere could this be more marked than crossing into Holland after living for ten months in France as we had then done. Crossing the border on water emphasised the dramatic change even more by injecting us abruptly into rural Holland, the kind of transition denied the air and train traveller, often the motorist as well.

We did not know the country well: a few days in Amsterdam for both of us and, for me, travels through western Holland as an undergraduate in the Thirties. I had also spent several bleak and uncomfortable winter months in southern Holland during the war, an experience that was often boring, occasionally exciting and very nearly terminal. To be immersed in the countryside and villages of pastoral Holland was, therefore, immensely interesting and refreshing for both of us, and a startling contrast to what we had become familiar with during the previous months. After France the 'Dutchness' of everything had the impact of discovery, a discovery that kept unfolding as we came to know the country better. I never ceased to enjoy the human scale of the tidy little towns, the diminutive brick houses, the large uncurtained, lace-trimmed windows filled with plants, the brick streets, the narrow canals with their wooden lift bridges and the inevitable windmills saved from the past.

These little country towns, many of them ancient, gave me constant visual pleasure as did the rich green landscape around them, stretching to the horizon in all directions. Lacking the hills and variety of other lands, Holland has an attraction of an entirely different sort. Farming and water dominate this horizontal, almost two-dimensional world. Canals, small and large are everywhere, cleaving the emerald fields in long, straight, shimmering cuts to disappear in converging lines like a lesson in perspective. Wherever one looked the views were wide and open, the green land playing almost a minor role in what was more skyscape than landscape. In Holland, as on the Canadian prairies, the sky holds the attention in a way it never does in places more closed in by hills and trees and it is no surprise that the sky played such a leading role in much of Dutch landscape painting. Beneath this wide expanse of blue or cloudy grey, a lush, verdant carpet stretches into the distance, marked only here and there by the staccato black and white of grazing cows, an isolated clump of trees, a great red-roofed barn and often, far away, a sail sliding silently across the fields. It has a calm, restful, almost abstract quality that acted on me like a tonic.

We pointed *Lionel* north into this flat green land, first down the Ijssel River past Arnhem, Zutphen and Deventer before turning on to a canal near Zwolle to continue north through Hasselt and Blokzijl, one of the few fortified towns in this part of Holland. Once on the shore of the Zuiderzee, it now lies far from open water, the reclaimed land of the Noordoost Polder standing between it and what remains of the old inland sea. Blokzijl is a delightful place, seventeenth and eighteenth-century buildings forming a gabled pink boundary wall around the generous basin at the centre of the old town. It was our first taste of such a place. We found it captivating, and were tempted to stay longer against the cobbled, tree-lined quay in the quiet little harbour but after a day or so, with some regret, we left Blokzijl behind and headed north.

At the much reduced speed demanded on Dutch canals we wandered slowly north towards Friesland, passing shortly through an unusually beautiful stretch of canal. It was unusual for its mature trees, its gentle meandering course between the bright green of manicured lawns and immaculate old houses, many sporting crisply sculpted roofs of thatch. Fresh paint sparkled everywhere, from the houses and the boats each possessed, tethered in neat little harbours of their own. On the canal, boats went past carrying handsome smiling people and, on the brick towpath a rolling line of more handsome, happy figures pedalled past. It was warm, the sun shone bright in a cerulean sky, the fresh washed green of early summer was all about. Nature could have done no better and people, houses, bicycles and boats all fell neatly into place. By coincidence or magic plan the different elements had come together at this very place and time in some rare conjunction to flash one brief glimpse of something almost outside real life. It all seemed too good to be true, the air so laden with a sense of happiness and well being that it might have been a travel poster bursting into life. Or could it be, perhaps, a peek at some unattainable utopian ideal? Whatever it was, the experience made such an impression on me that I found it hard accepting it as the mundane reality of Holland on a pleasant Sunday afternoon.

As we navigated our way through Holland, I was making great use of the excellent Dutch waterways maps, a bundle of which I'd bought at Lobith. I examined the relevant ones carefully before starting each day and it was certainly necessary. Holland is not like France where lock sizes, water depths and clearances vary little for any given canal and, although the first two are no problem in Holland where there are few locks and adequate water depths, the matter of clearance above the water can be critical. Bridges are, at times, very low, sometimes only a yard above the water. Some are moveable, some are not and some of the moveable ones only stir themselves at certain times on certain days. Routes, therefore, have to be planned carefully with the help of the maps which give information about bridge heights and types, but maps alone are not enough. One also needs an excellent little book which gives, amongst many other things, the opening times of every bridge over a navigable waterway in the entire country. Both this book and its companion volume* to do with regulations must be carried on all boats cruising Dutch waters. Both, alas, are only available in Dutch but a little work with a dictionary will usually extract the essential facts.

For many of the lift bridges a small toll is collected, especially in Friesland and the smaller towns. To do this efficiently, without delaying the moving boats, the Dutch have evolved a unique method. The bridge-keeper has a fishing-rod and line with a wooden clog fixed to the end. As boats pass his bridge he swings the clog with polished accuracy into the hands of a person on board. A coin is put in the clog which is retrieved by the bridge-keeper, all while the boat is in motion. It is a charming and ingenious solution to the humdrum business of collecting tolls with a little touch of sport thrown in for good measure.

---

* *Almanak voor Watertoerisme*

Friesland

Travelling steadily north through the gentle, watery landscape we arrived at last in Sneek (pronounced 'snake'), right in the middle of the Friesian lake district, much favoured by Dutch boating enthusiasts, most of whom, it appeared, had also decided to join us there in the month of July. The town was 'wall to wall' boats but luck was with us and we sidled into a spot between two lift bridges on a narrow canal, part of the intricate route through Sneek for all boats going north or south. We happened to be opposite a distillery making the Friesian fire water, Beerenburg, related to the Dutch gin, Genever, and flavoured with herbs to give it a uniquely bitter taste, but our mooring's main feature was boats, hundreds of boats.

When the two lift bridges were operating at each end of the canal, there was a constant flow of boats, first one way, then the other, in dense spasmodic processions, tooting their horns to alert the bridge-keepers: wooden dinghies, rubber inflatables, fancy plastic yachts, towed trains of little sailing-boats full of kids, windsurfers, lovely old wooden sailing craft, scruffy steel barges, motor-cruisers from minuscule to gross, sometimes a giant tour boat barely squeezing past, ungainly craft incredibly navigating the town's canals under sail and weird creations one can only describe as homemade dream boats. This almost endless two-way shuffling parade stopped only when the bridges closed and calm, thankfully, returned to the canal.

Watching all this at close hand brought respect for the skill of the Dutchmen in charge of these boats. It is difficult enough threading a boat through congested traffic in the narrow canals of Dutch towns but with wind added, as it often was, one could expect, at least, frayed tempers if not worse but I never saw anything like that. The boats were handled with unusual skill, in the circumstances, a skill that perhaps comes naturally to a people growing up in a land where water and boats must enter their lives at an early age. But it was more than skill. There was also a concern for others which is far from common and a *bonhomie* towards the world at large that was almost overwhelming. The Dutch are great wavers, perhaps the greatest wavers of western Europe. Every boat that passed was full of them, waving their summer away and we replied in kind. But as the days went by our waves became so perfunctory with constant repetition that Melodie even proposed an oscillating cardboard hand to relieve us of the chore.

At the busiest times there was almost incessant tooting of horns in our little boat-filled canal but, in one of the quieter moments, *Lionel* decided to add its own considerable voice to the general chorus. I had been making some electrical repairs behind the instrument panel, precariously propped up at the time with its ganglia of wires exposed. While somewhere else on the boat, I suddenly heard our horn take off on a powerful sustained note that blasted down the canal, ricocheted off the hard brick walls and turned every head in *Lionel*'s direction. This horn was not like the little things on other boats but had an authoritative, piercing, *basso* tone designed to spring lock-keepers from their TV sets over a mile away. In the confined space of the Sneek canal, it was an electrifying noise. Feeling very much the centre of attention I rushed to the wheelhouse, found the cause and brought the shattering intrusion to an end.

The sojourn in Sneek was a welcome pause in our travels. It was an attractive old place criss-crossed by canals and narrow streets with a wonderfully fanciful watergate guarding its heart. We explored the town on foot, visited its excellent small museum, bought food in its market, spent too much in its ships' chandlers, bicycled its outskirts and established closer contact with its citizens. But Sneek is but a tiny urban outcrop in a great green sea of pasture land and, walking its streets, this fact was often brought forcibly to one's attention by the extraordinarily acrid vapours of animal manure that wafted through the town from time to time, so concentrated and so pungent it seemed like an alien invasion of the streets and quite unlike the gentler smells of any farm I have known. It was, I suppose, an appropriate reminder of all those black and white cows out there beyond the town which were, after all, Friesland's principal resource.

It was during these wanderings that I began to realise something about the Dutch that I had not fully absorbed before. Although I had earlier been struck by their unusual good looks I had thought this more in the eye of the observer than the observed. But as we travelled through Friesland it was frequently confirmed, corroborated by Melodie and acquired the status of fact. Whatever the reason, this flowering of fine features and tall, trim figures was obvious enough. It was especially true of the young and tantalisingly so with the girls who, in those warm summer days, were more obviously and delightfully what they are than in the heavy wrappings of winter. Far more remarkably, however, the old had kept their figures and good looks as well with hardly a pot belly visible among these lean, vigorous, straight-backed bicycle-riders. And perhaps this is one of their secrets. Holland is a country of bicycle-riders, millions of them, their flat country lending itself to leg-driven wheels. They start young and keep going all their lives, battling the ever-present wind. It may not explain why they are such a handsome people but must have a lot to do with their manifest good health.

By the time we reached Sneek, it had been three years since the purchase of *Lionel* and the last time its hull had been cleaned, inspected, repaired and tarred, too long a time for an old boat. Holland is a barge country with all the resources available for their care at costs greatly lower than those in France and it was partly for this reason that we'd made the long journey north. That I finally decided to have the work on the hull done in Sneek, mainly a yacht town, was the discovery of a long-established small boatyard, run by succeeding generations of the same family. It had the required equipment, was able to take the boat in two weeks' time and gave me confidence the job would be properly done. Arrangements were, therefore, made to bring *Lionel* to this yard in the middle of August and, having two weeks to spare, we set off to explore more of Friesland.

Friesland is quite special in its way, special for its lake district scenery so valued by the Dutch, for its history and culture, for its separate language and its political aspirations, Friesland being the only Dutch province with daring dreams of independence. For the most part it is fenland country dotted with lakes, water never far away in any direction, even from the surface of the ground which is too wet for grain but can produce five crops of hay in one good growing season and provides the rich pastureland on which the sheep and Friesian cows prosper. It is a land of sweeping flat green fields, lakes, vast expanses of sky, enormous barns, snug little villages, black and white cows and sails. The great barns are the landmarks of this horizontal landscape, the largest objects to be seen, their red tiled roofs, sheltering man and beast, almost reaching to the ground. Not so long ago, their winter heat came mainly from the animals themselves and the farm family spent their night sitting upright on beds in wooden cupboards, believing that blood drained from their heads and better health resulted.

Nowadays the farm people are still the backbone of proud Friesland, a friendly rivalry between the towns of the province also helping to knit it together and preserve the strong spirit of the region. In the summer there are highly competitive races between sailing barges, one each from the five major towns, and, in the winter, when conditions permit, there are skating competitions on the frozen canals. The most important of these, a marathon race of a hundred and twenty-four miles between the eleven historical towns of Friesland, was watched in 1985 by over a million spectators along the route where farmers laid straw and carpets down at crossing points to prevent the paved surfaces blunting the skates of two hundred and twenty-four competitors. That race was won by Evert van Benthem in the record time of six hours and forty-six minutes at the remarkable average speed of just over eighteen miles per hour. When presented his medal by Queen Beatrix, it is said 'he thanked his Queen, saluted the cheering crowd and then went home to milk his cows'.

Heading north-east from Sneek, Friesland seemed to be surpassing itself in wetness. The weather was determined to remain awful as it had been and would be for the entire summer. The wind blew steadily from the west pushing herds of jostling grey clouds over the sodden fields and splashing rain down in short bursts, more unsettling, in their way, than an all-day soak. We moored for the night in a driving shower beside an unbelievably green but saturated pasture. The next day was even worse, so we remained water-bound, glumly watching the rain smash against the wheelhouse windows. There was water everywhere one looked: in the dark-brown depths of the canal, in the gathering puddles on the fields, in the sheets of it cascading from above. It was almost an underwater experience but the streaming windows revealed a kind of life still struggling on outside in the canal. Little wooden dinghies drifted past in the pouring rain, sails drooping and huddled, drenched figures in the stern, stubbornly sailing waterlogged open boats against all common sense. But it was summer, holiday time, and the determined Dutch sailed on, cold, rain and soaking clothes be damned.

The following day, under a dark grey overcast sky, we travelled east on the Princess Margaret Canal, a broad water highway running across the northern provinces and, with its extensions, linking Holland's inland sea, the Ijsselmeer to Groningen, the German canal system and the North Sea near Emden. It was much used by barges and, although more attractive than such canals usually are, didn't offer many things of interest apart from the incongruous sight of a large 'cargoliner' under construction in the tiny village of Gerkesklooster, towering over everything but the church spire. The sheer bulk of the immense ocean-going 1,500-tonner sitting on props against the background of the diminutive village houses was an odd juxtaposition of different scales, like a beach picnic suddenly joined by a whale.

Groningen, in the north-east corner of Holland just outside Friesland, is the largest town in the region and probably the largest north of Amsterdam. Winding our way into its centre, through numerous lift bridges all operated by one man who rode from one to the other on a bicycle, was a time-consuming business. And, as we now could expect in any Dutch town, boats lined the quays without a break, not yachts or cruisers as in Sneek, but mostly private barges, many being lived on. As we reached the centre with not a mooring in sight, the only remaining option was to moor alongside another boat, never a popular one with us. Moored this way it is often difficult getting Joss across to the quay for walks, it is almost impossible to disembark a scooter, it is inconvenient carrying heavy shopping-bags over an obstacle course of railings, ropes, hoses etc. and there is a certain loss of privacy for both boats. But it was tie to another boat or return to the country, so we moored to an immaculate barge whose Dutch owner graciously gave his permission.

It had been a long day and Joss was understandably keen to sniff the green grass on the quay a little distance away. So off we went down the narrow deck of the neighbouring barge to cross over at the bow as barge courtesies dictate. Here there was a miscellaneous pile of ropes and hoses which we had to cross before going down the other side and up a ramp to the shore. But things didn't quite work out the way I'd intended. Joss was hard pressed and perhaps a little confused in her mind about what was boat and what was shore. Right there, on a coil of rope in the bow of our neighbour's meticulously kept barge, Joss did what she had to do. Shouting my dismay, I yanked her hastily to the quay, calling to Melodie for help over my shoulder. Always prompt in an emergency, she came running and by the time Joss and I had returned from our now largely pointless walk, all had been restored to its original pristine state, the owner happily ignorant of the whole affair.

Groningen proved to be a disappointment, based on the superficial judgements of a very brief stay. The weather was bad, our mooring not much better and a large part of the town nearby was enduring the trauma of dusty reconstruction. To aggravate matters we had suffered through a very expensive but absolutely dreadful meal in a phony, Frenchified restaurant where a noisy wedding party obliterated conversation and the waiter's idea of satisfying our request for a German wine was to suggest adding a little sweet syrup to the inferior and excessively dry house wine! Apart from that the town seemed unkempt, lacking even the cohesion one had come to expect in this ordered land. Perhaps Groningen had suffered from some renovation in the recent past that had removed or harmed what had remained of the city's old core, for it now seemed empty, lacking focus. It may well be that in other circumstances our reactions would have been more favourable but there it was and, after a few days, we returned along the same canals to arrive in Leeuwarden, the capital of Friesland, just north of Sneek.

Sooner or later the weather had to improve and it did. The sun, which we had almost decided must be a non-Dutch phenomenon, shone down between the clouds to raise our spirits and welcome us to the old town. Surprisingly the quays of Leeuwarden were less crowded than other places, even the lovely lagoon in a park at the city's heart having relatively few boats, and it was there that we tied up. It was a wonderfully peaceful place, grass sloping gently up from the water's edge to a little hill, a few people strolling by under large trees and ducks padding about on the grass or drifting silently by in little convoys. Boats were even unobtrusively provided for with bollards, garbage bins and a water tap. The only change from the peaceful atmosphere of the park came on a Sunday afternoon when, in a bandstand beside a pool on the far side of the little hill, Rosie Vanderstoep's European Dance Band enthusiastically turned out journeyman jazz for three hours. That may sound dreadful but it wasn't. I like jazz and Rosie plus his five helpers were good enough to make listening to them enjoyable, first close at hand and later from a distance, as the music, muted by the trees, drifted rhythmically down to *Lionel* in the lagoon.

It was in Leeuwarden that the Dutch restaurant trade partially recovered some of its reputation struck such a grievous blow in Groningen. The Dutch are great vegetable eaters and we were to find out for the first time what that can mean. The main dish was sweetbread, its *béarnaise* sauce being the only hint of France. All the rest was unmistakably Dutch. Not only was the sweetbread garnished with ample little piles of kiwi fruit, sea grass, lettuce and finely shredded cucumber in sweet vinegar dressing but the entire surface of our table was occupied by dishes holding a veritable market garden of other nutritious delights; rice, fennel in egg batter, small cobs of corn, beans, carrots, seaweed, broccoli and two kinds of potatoes: counting it all, no less than twelve different members of the vegetable family and one of them appeared twice!

The boatyard

Most boatyards, especially those dealing with barges, are cluttered, rust-stained wastelands with nothing green in sight. Yacht boatyards are usually tidier and cleaner but they also tend to be hard-surfaced deserts with few redeeming natural features. The boatyard run by the van der Meulen family in Sneek was not at all like either of these, resembling far more what one might expect at the business end of the better kind of yacht club with a dash of rural Holland thrown in. Located on a side canal at the outskirts of the town, it was a secluded, out-of-the-way place of grass, tall trees, paved walks and wooden sheds on either side of a little inlet off the canal. It was in one of these sheds that the van der Meulens built the traditional sailing craft they had such a reputation for and in another, on the other side of the inlet, a long line of their brightly varnished boats rocked gently back and forth in the dim light of their boathouse.

Lionel's arrival at the boatyard on a Sunday in high wind threatened to be troublesome. Small boats lined the canal and one side of the little basin. They all looked delicate and to be avoided at all costs by a heavy steel bruiser like *Lionel*, so I poked the bow into the basin hoping for the best, there being little else that I could do. Fortunately, an English-speaking Dutchman appeared from out of his boat, which he moved, and helped us moor where it had been. Even with his help, it was tricky enough in the tiny space, further complicated by the steel hoisting tracks somewhere below in the water, one of which I heard our propeller nick as we manoeuvred into place.

Over the following two weeks we would come to know this boatyard well. It was a peaceful, relaxed place: grass, boats, trees, water, people, all coming together in a pleasant mix far removed from the noises of the town. We sat on the grass in the sun whenever it made a rare appearance, we picknicked on the Dutch summer delicacy of lightly cured fresh herring and onions, we became friends with Peter, our helper on arrival, and Isabel, both then sharing the tiny cabin of the oldest known van der Meulen 'schouw' with their large black hairy dog. They were in Friesland for a sailing holiday but the dreadful weather had driven them finally to the sanctuary of the boatyard. I was sorry for their sakes but glad for ours because they were pleasant boatyard companions and without Peter's multi-lingual talents it is hard to imagine how we would have come to know Johannes van der Meulen, the boatyard owner, or how I would have fared in all the technical palaver arising from the work on *Lionel*.

The day following our arrival, *Lionel* was poled into position over two trolleys that ran on tracks sloping into the water. When tied in position, the boat was winched out sideways until there was over a yard clear beneath the keel, then wedged in place to prevent rocking. Once high and dry, *Lionel* became uninhabitable, especially for Joss whose ladder-climbing skills neither she nor we had any wish to test, and we moved into a hotel until our craft was waterborne again. The hull was then cleaned with a high-pressure hose, removing a three-year accumulation of green slime and dirt and, after drying, was ready for inspection.

Since the main point of the whole operation was to check the ability of the hull to keep the boat afloat and prepare it properly to do this, it was vital that its present state be known. This can be done in a number of ways, none of them a firm guarantee against surprises but some obviously better than others. You can look at the hull and perhaps get a few clues. You can go around tapping it with a hammer. You can drill it full of test holes. And you can have it tested with a sonic device, the most expensive and probably best method. I opted for the last and an independent inspector duly arrived to do the job. Selected spots all over the hull were ground down to bare steel, greased and tested sonically, revealing the astonishing result that the minimum steel thickness of 4.5mm was thicker by 1mm than the measurements taken by the same method three years before. A little uncertain about the meaning of this, I chose to accept the figures produced by the thorough Dutch inspection company rather than those arrived at earlier in the boatyard on the outskirts of Paris. Following the inspection, a welder did the few necessary repairs to hull and rudder post and some other essential bits of work. He, in turn, was followed by a specialist who arrived in a neat business suit and remained wearing it throughout his work of mending *Lionel*'s ravaged bronze propeller.

With work on the hull complete, it was given two coats of tar and eased gently back into the water. All that remained was some work on

the main engine and to test the newly installed depth sounder. This gave me an unexpected and unpleasant jolt when it registered widely varying and totally unbelievable depths of water below the boat, 20.6 metres, 0.1 metres, even 64.0 metres, whereas the truth was roughly 1.5 metres. In this deranged state the depth sounder was clearly quite useless but its cure would have to wait until the spring when *Lionel* would be out of the water again for further coats of tar.

Finally, a mechanic came to check over the main engine. Apart from new rubber seals for the injectors and a new oil line it needed little else even after its countless hours of running. And at my request, he also installed a new pump for emptying the engine sump during oil changes, leaving the old and quite useless one lying on the floor of the engine-room. Being a fairly orderly captain I wanted to get rid of it. Taking the old pump in my arms I started up the stairs to the wheelhouse where Melodie and the mechanic were having a chat. As I poked my head through the hatch, the pump emptied its entire unsuspected contents of black engine oil down my front, soaking me to the skin. Emerging streaked and dripping with the stuff, the now piebald skipper prompted merriment he thought a bit unseemly and retired quickly to the shower to deal with matters there. Diesel oil is dreadful stuff, dyed a dense black with carbon, almost as bad as printer's ink. There was nothing to be done but throw away my clothes and start scrubbing my weirdly dyed body. Although I scrubbed vigorously through the dermal layers the skin stubbornly remained a patchy indeterminate greenish grey. Only after days of similar treatment did my bodily envelope return to a semblance of its former self, though by then greatly the worse for wear.

By the end of August, our planned year in Europe was drawing to a close. *Lionel* would be left in Holland for the winter and returned to France the following spring to comply with Dutch regulations that only allow foreign boats a year's stay in the country. As yet unclear where to leave the boat, we had considered Amsterdam but found arrangements there unsatisfactory and security a very chancy business. So our thoughts turned to Sneek and the van der Meulen boatyard. I broached the matter to Johannes, the boss, a tall, thin, slightly stooped man in early middle age with reddish face and blond hair. He is an intelligent and thoughtful man, taciturn by nature yet blessed with charm and an easy smile that endears him to all who come to his boatyard. Being also a cautious man, he gave no immediate answer to my question but during the next day or so I saw him strolling around his boatyard carefully assessing if *Lionel* could be fitted in. Finally the answer was 'yes' and with relief we sat down to negotiate the price at a little conference in our wheelhouse with Johannes, Isabel, the indispensable Peter, Melodie and myself, wine and Beerenburg close at hand. Once settled the final preparations were made for laying up the boat.

Even in the south of France, as we discovered to our cost, winter can be a cruel season for a boat. In Holland conditions would be more severe and special precautions were taken so the boat would ride the winter through free of harm. Additional anti-freeze was added to the closed cooling system of the engine, water tanks were pumped dry, all pipes were drained by gravity, then blown out with compressed air, everything loose and vulnerable to frost, including the batteries, was removed from the boat for storage in a warm place, fuel was drained from Honda generators and scooter, the WC was pumped dry, all valves on gas, oil, water, heating and drainage lines were closed, furniture was covered, mattresses and sleeping bags left to air, all loose deck equipment stowed or tied down, tarpaulins were fixed over the wheelhouse and upper deck. Apart from ensuring that the boat would be inspected regularly and an electric heater turned on once in a while to dry the interior, there wasn't much more that we could do.

Laying up a boat is always a sad business. It brings to an end for a while a different and happy kind of life which must be put aside for the familiar even humdrum routines of normal existence. It is sad also for the boat, now deprived of its reason for being. There it sat, immobilised, trussed up like a badly wrapped package, its nerves turned off, its arteries choked, its muscles paralysed. It was really no longer a boat at all, but a lifeless, steel thing whose only remaining property was an ability to float. It could no longer move or even provide the limited comfort of a lowly houseboat. *Lionel* is only truly alive when its bows are slicing through the water, all its systems working and its bronze screw pushing it forward on some purposeful journey. It is a good feeling, what being on a boat is all about, and *Lionel* had been a good boat over the years since we first got to know one another, serving us well over hundreds of miles on canals and the biggest rivers of Europe, from Paris to the south of France, west almost to Toulouse and north again all the way to the top of Holland.

But what a change there had been in those three and a half years. The little barge first seen so long ago in the marina at St Cloud, although fundamentally sound had, in other ways, been in a sorry state, neglected, poorly equipped and abused by unfeeling hands. Over many long months it was restored and equipped in a process that touched every cranny and aspect of the old boat. It was a daunting challenge, its conclusion at times even hard to believe possible, but it was all made easier by the satisfaction that came with salvaging the retired tanker for a new and brighter future. The extraordinary boat Melodie and I had first seen was transformed, at last, into the comfortable and well-equipped barge it now is. Its rebirth had brought *Lionel* a new life and, I would like to think, a new self-respect as well. That in itself was a rewarding journey, long, rocky and never cheap, but immensely satisfying. It had come into its own again.

Over the years, *Lionel* has made a kind of repayment by carrying us faithfully through the water of so many canals and rivers, sometimes ice, and I hate to think how many locks. It has been the focus of our waterborne life, the scene of adventures and the source of great enjoyment. Like every member of its species *Lionel* has tossed our way a rich assortment of crises as machines are prone to do, sometimes trivial, often grave, once in a while catastrophic and always costly in cash, human stress or both. But, in all fairness, most of these sprang from owner-installed equipment or, too often, rampant 'human error': that convenient euphemism for sheer incompetence whose ghostly presence has stalked *Lionel*'s decks in the guise of journeymen mechanics, amateur artisans and, regrettably, the captain himself. It has been a long and dismal list, but the fundamental equipment of the boat will not be found on it for that has never failed: not the hull, not the engine, not the shaft and screw, not the steering. All these vital elements, the very essence of the boat's being, those things that keep it afloat and drive it along on a straight course, never let us down. They all performed magnificently and without complaint, compassionately tolerating the countless mistakes of its brand-new crew. The basic boat, owing much, no doubt, to its solid Dutch origins, pushed on, calm and unperturbed, through all the canals and swirling rivers. *Lionel* had proved to be a good boat, rugged, forgiving of abuse, responsive to wheel and throttle, with no bad habits and always a pleasure to be in charge of.

This willing companion of our travels had carried us so far, so ably and for so long, it was hard to part company even for the winter months. *Lionel* had become a warm familiar friend and an important part of our lives. Through this old barge we had seen France in a way we could not have done otherwise, it had brought us many new friends and, because of it, we had discovered a new, revitalised existence together. It was as if a new dimension had been added late in life when one wondered if any more would come along. In the regeneration of *Lionel*, also over sixty, we realised an unexpected renewal of ourselves.

Postscript

While exploring the waterways of north-eastern France in the early summer of 1987 Joss was aboard *Lionel* as always. She was then in her fifteenth year and beset occasionally with a troubling malady. When moored deep in the rural isolation of the Canal des Ardennes and far from any help the crisis we had long feared finally happened. The old trouble returned but Joss, weakened by age, had few resources left to fight it. She died in the middle of the night with Melodie and me close by during her final hours. Early the next morning we dug a grave at the edge of a field beside the canal and buried Joss wrapped in her favourite old blanket. Neither of us will ever forget our feelings as *Lionel* pulled slowly away from that sad mooring leaving the old friend and companion of our travels behind.

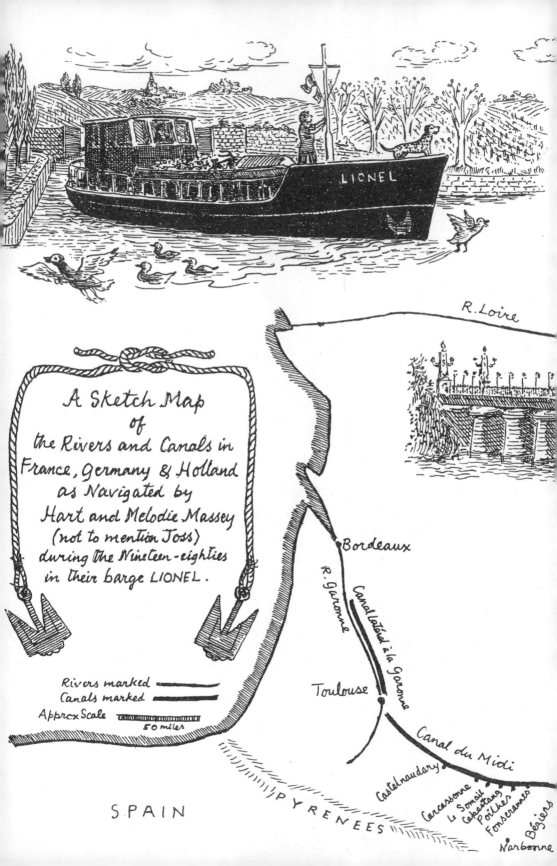

LIONEL

R. Loire

A Sketch Map
of
the Rivers and Canals in
France, Germany & Holland
as Navigated by
Hart and Melodie Massey
(not to mention Joss)
during the Nineteen-eighties
in their barge LIONEL.

Rivers marked
Canals marked
Approx Scale
50 miles

Bordeaux

R. Garonne

Canal Lateral à la Garonne

Toulouse

Canal du Midi

Castelnaudary

Carcassonne
L. Somail
Capestang
Poilhes
Fonserannes
Béziers
Narbonne

SPAIN

PYRENEES